Grammar Alive!

We gratefully acknowledge the contributions of the following members of the NCTE Assembly for the Teaching of English Grammar:

Paul E. Doniger
Helene Krauthamer
Johanna E. Rubba
Wanda Van Goor
Edith Wollin

ATEG

The NCTE Assembly for the Teaching of English Grammar aims to improve the teaching of grammar at all levels, from elementary school through college; to promote communication and cooperation among teachers, researchers, administrators, and others interested in the teaching of grammar; to provide an open forum in which advocates of all grammar theories, representing the broad spectrum of views of grammar and its teaching, can interact. Through its listserv, its conference, and its journal, *Syntax in the Schools,* ATEG offers educators information about grammar and suggestions for better ways to teach it. (For more information, visit ATEG's Web site at www.ateg.org.)

Grammar Alive!

A Guide for Teachers

Brock Haussamen

with Amy Benjamin, Martha Kolln, Rebecca S. Wheeler,
and members of NCTE's Assembly for the Teaching
of English Grammar

National Council of Teachers of English
1111 W. Kenyon Road, Urbana, Illinois 61801-1096

Chapter 5, "Non-Native Speakers in the English Classroom," was adapted from the book *Differentiated Instruction: A Guide for Middle and High School* by Amy Benjamin. This material is used with the permission of Eye on Education, Larchmont, New York, www.eyeoneducation.com.

Staff Editor: Bonny Graham

Interior Design: Doug Burnett

Cover Design: Barbara Yale-Read

NCTE Stock Number: 18720-3050

Library of Congress Cataloging-in-Publication Data

Haussamen, Brock.
   Grammar alive! : a guide for teachers / Brock Haussamen, with Amy Benjamin, Martha Kolln, and Rebecca Wheeler and members of NCTE's Assembly for the Teaching of English Grammar.
       p. cm.
Includes bibliographical references and index.
    ISBN 0-8141-1872-0
  1. English language—Grammar—Study and teaching. 2. English language—Study and teaching. 3. Language arts. I. Assembly for the Teaching of English Grammar. II. Title.
   LB1576.H3235 2003
   372.61—dc22

                           2003015117

Contents

II. On Grammar

Preface

The Assembly for the Teaching of English Grammar (ATEG) was born in the late 1980s with Edward Vavra's newsletter *Syntax in the Schools,* a forum for educators interested in the teaching of grammar and concerned about its neglect. The readers came together for the first ATEG conference at Dr. Vavra's institution, Shenandoah College in Winchester, Virginia, in 1989. Martha Kolln, from Pennsylvania State University, was elected president. In the years following, ATEG formally became an Assembly of the National Council of Teachers of English. Its members hold an annual conference in July at different institutions around the country. ATEG's goal has remained to encourage the effective teaching of grammar and to provide a forum for discussions about grammar teaching. The Assembly now publishes *Syntax in the Schools* as a refereed journal and has a Web site at www.ateg.org as well as an active listserv.

This guide is the product of many years of ATEG members' excitement about the possibilities for teaching grammar and their dismay that the subject has remained so bogged down in outdated ideas and approaches. In 1998, a committee began work on a report that evolved into this book.

The several authors of the book have both written portions of it and helped revise one another's work, so the collaboration has been a rich one. The introduction was written by Brock Haussamen, with revisions by Amy Benjamin. The three goals for the teaching of grammar, laid out in Chapter 1, were first formulated by Johanna Rubba; the discussions of the goals were written by Brock Haussamen. Most of the suggestions for methods and lessons in Chapters 2, 3, and 4 were first written by Amy Benjamin and Johanna Rubba. The methodology portion of Chapter 2, "Discovering Grammar through Language Variety," was written by Rebecca Wheeler. Chapter 5, "Non-Native Speakers in the English Classroom," was adapted from the book *Differentiated Instruction: A Guide for Middle and High School* by Amy Benjamin; it is used with the permission of the publisher, Eye on Education. I'm grateful to Miriam Moore and Christine Herron of Raritan Valley Community College for suggesting additions to this material. "Grammar Superstitions: The Never-Never Rules," Chapter 6, was written by Amy Benjamin. Chapter 7, "Diagramming Sentences," and the grammar glossary were prepared by Brock Haussamen with help from Martha Kolln, based on material from *Understanding English Grammar* by Martha Kolln and Robert Funk. Chapter 8, "An Overview of Linguistic Grammar," was written by Martha Kolln, who also contributed to the final edit of the whole manuscript. Chapters 3, 4, and the conclusion and portions of other sections were written by Brock Haussamen, who also organized and edited the entire book. The vignettes are signed by the authors. Additional ATEG members who commented on early drafts are Pam Dykstra, Loretta Gray, Edith Wollin, and Robert Yates. Finally, NCTE Senior Editor Zarina Hock and several anonymous readers made many helpful suggestions about additions to the original manuscript as well as improvements throughout the text.

Brock Haussamen
President, Assembly for the Teaching of English Grammar
Raritan Valley Community College

VIGNETTE: LANGUAGE ABOUT LANGUAGE: A MIDDLE SCHOOL GRAMMAR CLASS

The voices of the seventh and eighth graders in Mrs. Cahill's period 4 class spill out into the hall. Her students are often so boisterous that she feels a little chagrined: "What must people be thinking when they pass by this room sometimes during our Language Workshop?" she thinks.

One thing few people would think is that Mrs. Cahill is teaching grammar. There are no books, no exercises, no diagrams, no rules and maxims to learn. What the students bring to the lesson is their own language, the language they hear in their world. In today's lesson, Mrs. Cahill will teach sentence completeness and the difference between formal and informal registers. She uses the language of street signs. The students call out the street signs they know, beginning with the teacher's cues:

No Parking

Merge Left

The students burst into a torrent of street-sign language: Slippery When Wet; Wrong Way; Go Back; Dead End; No Outlet; Survey Crew Ahead; Last Exit Before Toll. Mrs. Cahill stops after writing twenty sign messages on the board.

"Are any of these complete sentences?" she asks. "Do any have both a subject and a verb?" When the students agree that the street signs do not represent complete sentences, Mrs. Cahill asks this: "What if you were to put the words *You should* in front of these signs? Which ones would become complete sentences then?" The kids test "You should . . . " against the signs.

"You should merge left."

"You should go back."

This is the teachable moment about the understood *you*-subject of commands.

"What other street signs give commands?" The students add "Stop" and "Yield" to their list. Mrs. Cahill explains that in the English language we have a convention that makes commands sound less bossy. "How would you say 'Stop' or 'Yield' more politely?" Of course, everyone says, "Please."

"Are there any other ways to sound polite when making a command? How would you say the other signs politely?"

The kids respond with "Please do not park here" and "Please turn around because you are going the wrong way."

The teacher points out that although the "please" form is the most obvious, we also can sound polite (formalize our register) by saying, "We would appreciate it if you would park elsewhere" or "It might be a good idea to merge left right about now." It's easy for kids to deduce that the formal register might not convey the needed imperative carried by the informal. When it comes to traffic signs, brevity is practical in more ways than one. "When you say it politely, it sounds like they don't have to do it right now," remarks one student. "When you just say 'do it,' they obey the sign."

"This is a dead end"; "This is the last exit before the toll." Mrs. Cahill asks if these statements are polite or impolite. The kids see that they are neither. These iterations are neutral in tone. "How would you make these signs dress down? How would you make them speak in an informal voice?"

"Wrong way, you idiot!"

"Wrong way . . . duh!"

"You better stop!"

"Hey, look at this view!"

Mrs. Cahill asks the students to make columns for phrases and clauses and then for declarative sentences and commands.

Mrs. Cahill's students think that her Language Workshop is fun, but they don't always see the connection between what they already know about language and what an English teacher cares about. So Mrs. Cahill prompts them. "What words have we used today that go in our Language About Language notes?" The students keep a section in their English notebook for terms such as *tone, command, subject, verb, complete sentence, phrase, clause, formal, informal.* Mrs. Cahill's Language Workshop has looked at advertising, slogans, movie quotations, sitcom titles, music, weather reports, dollar bills, CD jackets, and other examples of authentic language. The students' Language About Language pages continue to grow with examples and new terminology. And they never use a grammar book!

—Amy Benjamin

Introduction

A Broken Subject

At the start of this new millennium, throughout much of the K–12 English curriculum, grammar is a broken subject. If you find yourself just not knowing what to do about grammar—how to teach it, how to apply it, how to learn what you yourself were never taught—you are not alone. Grammar is often ignored, broken off altogether from the teaching of literature, rhetoric, drama, composition, and creative writing. Grammar is the skunk at the garden party of the language arts. Perhaps you've set aside time for labeling parts of speech, correcting errors, and modeling effective use of punctuation, but you may feel unmoored: you wonder whether the grammar you learned in school (what little there may have been) is sufficient or if the methods you learned by are up-to-date. And you certainly wouldn't be alone if you were embarrassed to reveal to your colleagues all that you don't know about grammar. Grammar feels like a frowning pedant reproaching you for not knowing enough about subject-verb agreement, for blithely ending sentences with prepositions, for splitting infinitives without even understanding what that means, for promiscuous use of commas and flagrant case violations. And, even if you speak and write with a confident tongue and well-schooled hand, you may tremble at the thought of trying to get your students to write complete sentences.

You are not alone. The obstacles to revitalizing the teaching of grammar are several. One is that our profession has lost sight of the connection between studying grammar and learning to read and write. As Robert J. Connors recounted in "The Erasure of the Sentence," our interest in analyzing sentences has faded since the 1970s. Today it is the *process* of writing, along with originality, authenticity, and personal writing, that we value. The change has left sentence-level work—even such proven approaches as sentence combining—in shadow. We're not comfortable encouraging students to be original and authentic one minute and then assigning them exercises in sentence structure the next. Many English departments, and highly respected English teachers, argue forcefully that sentence-level work is mechanical, behavioristic, antihumanistic, and, most scorn-worthy of all, boring.

Another obstacle to revitalizing the role of grammar is the tension between the traditional teaching of grammar and the varieties of language that our students speak in their homes. It's understandable if you feel on shaky ground at the thought of setting up rules about correct and incorrect English. After all, who are you to declare that *your* brand of English should trump anyone else's? One of the foremost goals of the curriculum is to broaden the Western canon, fostering multiculturalism, not undermining it. How does living harmoniously in a pluralistic society square with the mandate to teach, model, and prefer the variety of English spoken easily by the dominant culture? On the other hand, we acknowledge our duty to equip students with the keys they will need to open doors that might be closed to them on the basis of their speech, not to mention their writing. English, like almost all languages, has a prestige dialect: the language of power is used for business, education, and government. The opposing force is the value that we place on treasuring the diversity of American subcultures, and what is more intimate to these subcultures than their language? You may well feel caught in the middle between these obligations, and there is no easy way to find a balance.

These two tensions—between the traditional teaching of grammar and the goals of both confident writing and the culturally inclusive classroom—entail complex issues and valid charges. This guide from the Assembly for the Teaching of English Grammar does not analyze or deny the charges. Instead it is a proposal for overcoming both conflicts by integrating grammar into the multicultural reading/writing classroom. It asks and proposes answers to several questions:

- How can we teach grammar to support learning in all language skills?
- How can we teach grammar so that students discover its rules and principles on their own instead of hearing us impose those rules and principles on them?
- How can we teach grammar so that we strengthen rather than undermine our efforts to honor the voices and cultures of all students?
- How can we teach grammar so that the knowledge it provides can help learners feel confident about their own language and appreciate the languages of others?

We must answer these questions because, despite the rejection of traditional grammar teaching, grammar does not go away. It appears in almost all language arts texts. Almost all schoolchildren are assigned lessons on the parts of speech and the basic rules—even if they do not understand them, do not remember them, and cannot apply them. We have a nagging sense that we may not be delivering the full package when we disregard grammar. But we don't know where to begin. You are probably reading this book because you want to teach grammar or have been required to do so. The education courses you took, however, probably neglected grammar and linguistics, so you may feel that you have little choice but to follow the mostly dry, mechanical treatments of grammar, the "no-no's" of the rules and errors, that have changed little in the textbooks and are the reason so many believe that grammar should instead be shelved.

Two Kinds of Grammar

The underlying reason that grammar hangs on in the curriculum is that we realize that knowledge about language is valuable. Actually, the term *grammar* refers to two kinds of knowledge about language. One is subconscious knowledge, the language ability that children develop at an early age without being taught. As children begin to talk, as they become able to form sentences, their brains are forming their "grammar circuits" automatically. The other kind of knowledge is the conscious understanding of sentences and texts that can help students improve their reading and writing abilities by building on that subconscious knowledge. This conscious understanding includes knowing the parts of sentences and how they work together, knowing how sentences connect with one another to build meaning, and understanding how and why we use language in different ways in different social situations.

In teaching grammar in school, we are not really teaching grammar at all: children learn that automatically; rather, we are teaching students *about* grammar, and we are hoping to bring them the added confidence and clarity that go with any knowledge that strengthens skills and deepens understanding. That we are "teaching *about* grammar" is an insight that comes to us from work in linguistics over the last century. This book includes some of that work.

The problem with school grammar has not been grammar itself as much as it has been the way grammar is usually taught. Instead of helping students to focus on real literature or on the actual paper they are writing, traditional grammar pedagogy requires students to divert their attention to the isolated and often contrived sentences in a textbook. It encourages students—and teachers—to believe that the authority for Standard English is that separate book of rules rather than literature and the language of those with power and prestige in the living culture. It focuses on errors instead of on the understanding of language. Some teachers still lament that they can teach comma rules or subject-verb agreement at length only to find that their students continue to make the errors. But many other teachers do understand that writing is an exceedingly complex cognitive and social task. The reduction of conventional errors takes a great deal of experience in reading, in writing, and in talking about reading and writing. Formal grammar is a tool for talking about and thinking about sentences; it is not, by itself, a tool for making errors go away (as Constance Weaver emphasizes in *Teaching Grammar in Context* and in her other books, listed in the "Sources and Resources" section at the end of the book).

Let's consider the traditions that stand behind the way formal grammar has been taught out of the textbook. We do this to understand how grammar education has become what it is today. Until the modern era, the teaching of grammar rules was primarily a method for teaching a *foreign* language. The emphases on the parts of speech, the dissection of sentences, and the correct answers to exercises all have ancient and medieval roots in grammar as a method for teaching a second language. (Brock Haussamen has traced the history of many of our traditional grammar rules and terms in *Revising the Rules: Traditional Grammar and Modern Linguistics;* see "Sources and Resources.") Grammar books were first used to teach Homeric Greek to non-Greeks, then Latin to non-Romans. Then, in eighteenth-century England, educators who believed that they needed to correct the "flawed" language of working-class children and adults adopted the same classical tools and models (they fussed, for example, that perhaps sentences should not end with prepositions because they never did so in Latin), and we have been using the same approaches ever since.

The result has been that we have traditionally taught grammar to students without appreciating the fact that they already have a full grammar system—an ability to organize language meaningfully—in their heads. Consequently, the grammar of the classroom has often seemed to students like so much unnecessary jargon they have to learn about a language they already know. Or, if students are dialect speakers for whom mainstream English is puzzling and strange, traditional grammar, with all its rules and exceptions (do you remember all the exceptions to the subject-verb agreement rule?), is not much help. Today, we know more about language, we know more about how brains learn, and we need to reorient ourselves about grammar.

The time may be propitious for a new approach to grammar because attitudes toward traditional grammar and mechanical correctness have been shifting in recent decades. The English profession in general and the National Council of Teachers of English in particular began to reduce the emphasis on the traditional teaching of grammar in the 1960s and 1970s as research began to show that teaching grammar in isolation failed to improve writing and only cut into time better spent on fluency, process, and voice. In the 1990s, pockets of revitalized and genuinely useful grammar appeared in books—the most popular ones by Constance Weaver, Martha Kolln, and Rei Noguchi—that integrated linguistic grammar and traditional grammar and showed teachers ways to apply this modernized grammar in the classroom. But a new trend looms. High-stakes testing threatens to bring back grammar in its most reactionary and ineffective form—the monotonous drilling on errors and parts of speech. We can only hope that standardized testing prompts all English educators to take a closer look at the new insights into the teaching of grammar if for no other reason than to avoid taking a giant step backwards.

Grammar Alive! consists of two parts. Part I focuses primarily on strategies for teaching grammar. Part II focuses more on grammar itself and information about grammar that you might find useful.

Part I opens with "Three Goals for Teaching Grammar," goals with equal priority that enable grammar to take on a balanced and positive role in the language arts classroom. Chapter 2, "Discovering Grammar," discusses such terms as *Standard English* and offers approaches for introducing students to the presence of grammar in the full range of spoken and written language. Chapter 3, "Teaching the Language of Grammar," discusses new approaches to describing the parts of speech and to helping students understand and apply them. Chapter 4, "Flexing the Students' Sentence Sense," focuses on how much students already know about sentences and how they can apply that knowledge to improve their writing and their appreciation of literature. Chapter 5 is "Non-Native Speakers in the English Classroom"; this section discusses some of the differences between English and the other languages that students may be speaking, and it covers many suggestions for helping such students in the English classroom. Vignettes—narrations of classroom grammar lessons—are integrated into or follow each of these chapters.

Part II, "On Grammar," covers information about grammar that can clarify your own understanding of the subject and give you further options in the classroom. Chapter 6, "Grammar Superstitions: The Never-Never Rules," discusses such supposed errors as the split infinitive that you may not be sure about. Chapter 7, "Diagramming Sentences," provides a short guide to traditional sentence diagrams. Chapter 8, "An Overview of Linguistic Grammar," is a full introduction to the current linguistic descriptions of word classes and sentence structure.

In the conclusion, you will find a grammar glossary that will help you refresh your understanding of exactly what all the grammar terms mean, and it includes plenty of examples. An annotated list of sources and resources in print and on the Internet will help you find further information about the teaching of grammar.

I Grammar in the Classroom

1 Three Goals for Teaching Grammar

The three goals presented in this chapter are intended—in words borrowed from the introduction to the NCTE/IRA *Standards for the English Language Arts*—to "embody a coherent, professionally defensible conception of how a field can be framed for purposes of instruction" (viii). They state outcomes in grammar instruction that include a wide range of abilities related to grammar, from the ability to write Standard English to an understanding of language prejudice.

You may find them ambitious and idealistic, and they are. These goals are intended to provide direction and context for grammar instruction up through the completion of high school. You may have asked yourself what you can possibly teach your students about a complex subject like grammar during the year they will be in your class. You may not know what grammar, if any, your students have been taught or will be taught by other teachers. When we as teachers are not sure whether grammar is included throughout our curriculum, we tend to stick to the basics—the basic writing errors, the basic parts of speech. For students, the result is often tedious repetition. In such a disconnected grammar curriculum, students lose out on much of grammar that is important and exciting.

In contrast, these three grammar goals summarize three strands of a comprehensive grammar curriculum. In a language arts curriculum that included these strands, students would not only develop a command of Standard English, but they would also understand at a basic level the role that language structure plays in literature, the way language changes through time and in different social situations, and the fact that all languages and language varieties have grammatical structure. Ambitious? Certainly. But the following chapters will each discuss ways that you and your students can work toward these achievements.

About the Three Grammar Goals

Goal A

Every student, from every background, will complete school with the ability to communicate comfortably and effectively in both

Goals for Teaching Grammar

Goal A
Every student, from every background, will complete school with the ability to communicate comfortably and effectively in both spoken and written Standard English, with awareness of when use of Standard English is appropriate.

Goal B
Every student will complete school with the ability to analyze the grammatical structure of sentences within English texts, using grammatical terminology correctly and demonstrating knowledge of how sentence-level grammatical structure contributes to the coherence of paragraphs and texts.

Goal C
Every student will complete school with an understanding of, and appreciation for, the natural variation that occurs in language across time, social situation, and social group. While recognizing the need for mastering Standard English, students will also demonstrate an understanding of the equality in the expressive capacity and linguistic structure among a range of language varieties both vernacular and standard, as well as an understanding of language-based prejudice.

> spoken and written Standard English, with awareness of when
> use of Standard English is appropriate.

"Standard English" is the variety of English that many people in the economic mainstream and predominant social culture of the United States speak and write. Sometimes it is called Mainstream American English. Standard English is the variety of English that grammar books describe. It is standard not in the sense that it is better English than other varieties but in the sense that it is the widely recognized and codified version of English.

A more precise name for it is Edited American English—"Edited" since it is the version of our language that writers and editors of books and periodicals follow, and "American" in that it is the language written in the United States as opposed to England, where some spellings (*color, colour; airplane, aeroplane*), vocabulary (*mailbox, pillar box; gasoline, petrol)*, and usage (e.g., the deletion of the definite article, as in *She is in hospital*) are different.

Standard English is sometimes referred to also as the Language of Wider Communication, a name reflecting the belief that when people in the United States talk or write to people other than friends and family in another part of the country, this is the language that is most likely to be the "common currency." It is the language variety that the stranger in an office at the other end of the telephone or letter or e-mail will probably be the most familiar with.

But the notion of a *standard* language raises some questions that are obvious if you think about the word for a moment. *Standard* for whom? Everywhere? Always? In all details? Standard English is not a single, pure type of English, although some people like to think that it is so specific and so solid, like a yardstick made of gold, that we can compare it with samples of language and find out easily whether the samples fall short.

For instance, there is an important category of English known as Informal Standard English. The *American Heritage Dictionary* uses the label "informal" to designate "words that are acceptable in conversation with friends and colleagues [but that] would be unsuitable in the formal prose of an article written for publication in the journal of a learned society" (3rd edition, xxxvii). *Wish list* is an example of Informal Standard English.

In addition to this category, there are what linguists designate as regional standards, the entirely acceptable, clear, and "normal" ways that people talk in specific geographical regions. Regional standards may differ in some ways from the specifications in the grammar books of Edited American English. And yet to ask whether, for that reason, a certain regional phrase is "correct" makes no sense. Martha Kolln and Robert Funk illustrate this point well:

> Imagine that your job is to record the speech of Pennsylvanians. In Pittsburgh and its surrounding areas, you hear such sentences as "My car needs fixed" and "My hair needs washed" and "Let the door open." In Philadelphia, three hundred miles to the east, you hear instead "My car needs to be fixed" and "My hair needs washing" and "Leave the door open." As a linguist are you going to judge one group's speech as grammatical and the other's as ungrammatical? Of course not. You have no basis for doing so. . . . Many of the sentences that get labeled "ungrammatical" are simply usages that vary from one dialect to another, what we sometimes call regionalisms. (7)

So keep in mind that "Standard English" is a concept with some flexibility to it. It has its gray areas. Nonetheless, clearly an essential goal of education is for students to gain as much mastery of Standard English as they can. Goal A recognizes that students, no matter which language variety they speak and hear at home, will be expected to use the codes and conventions of Standard English in many situations. In the workplace, a written report or memorandum will require Standard English, as will most conversations with supervisors. Outside of the workplace, students-turned-adults should be able to communicate with professional people such as lawyers or doctors in Standard English. The study of grammar is by no means the only, or even the primary, method for achieving this goal. More important, as English teachers know, are generous amounts of reading, speaking, listening, and writing. But students need a conscious knowledge of grammar so that they can talk about sentences and about the conventions of Standard English.

Goal B

> Every student will complete school with the ability to analyze the grammatical structure of sentences within English texts, using grammatical terminology correctly and demonstrating knowledge of how sentence-level grammatical structure contributes to the coherence of paragraphs and texts.

This goal emphasizes the value of understanding the basic components of and relationships between sentences. This understanding is valuable not only for helping writers understand the conventions of Standard English but also for helping both writers and readers understand how sentences work together to create coherent, meaningful text. Often, you may have found yourself teaching students about the parts of speech and the word groups that make up sentences only to find that neither you nor the students could put that knowledge to much use in writing a clear essay or in appreciating literature. The grammar lesson is finished, the work sheets are handed in, the students open up their literature books, and the grammar is left behind. Goal B is about not leaving grammar behind. Chapters 3 and 4 focus on these topics of terminology and coherence.

Goal C

> Every student will complete school with an understanding of, and appreciation for, the natural variation that occurs in language across time, social situation, and social group. While recognizing the need for mastering Standard English, students will also demonstrate an understanding of the equality in the expressive capacity and linguistic structure among a range of language varieties both vernacular and standard, as well as an understanding of language-based prejudice.

We use the term *language variety* in this book instead of the word *dialect*. In linguistics, *dialect* refers to any variety of a language in which the use of grammar and vocabulary identifies the regional or social background of the user. African American Vernacular English, now generally referred to as African American English, is a dialect of English. For linguists, so is Standard English. But the word *dialect* carries some serious baggage. For many people, and perhaps for you as well, dialects are "bad" English—nothing neutral about them—and it seems contradictory to think of Standard English as a dialect. So to minimize the confusion, language specialists recommend using the term *language variety* in its place. Language variety refers to any socially or regionally distinctive pattern of grammar and vocabulary within the larger language. This is the practice we are following in this ATEG guide.

Goal C includes the word *vernacular:* "a range of language varieties both vernacular and standard." *Vernacular* is both a noun and an adjective that refers to the everyday language of a region and to everyday language in general. Sometimes it is used to distinguish between "plain" conversational language and "flowery" literary language. Also, as here, it distinguishes between ordinary speech and formal Standard English (in either writing or speaking). "Me'n Jim'r goin' over his house after school" is an example of the vernacular of an eighth-grade boy who is speaking to his friends.

Although *vernacular* does not carry the same intensely negative connotations that the term *dialect* does, it often brings out our assumptions, perhaps unconscious ones, about "better" and "worse" language. It may be hard to resist the belief that a sentence in the vernacular such as the example in the previous paragraph is a sloppy and careless sentence—one that, understandably, people may say in the rush of conversation but that nonetheless would be "better" if the pronoun case were corrected—*I* instead of *me*—if the *to* were added after *over,* and if the pronunciation were clearer.

Goal C asks that we look at such examples of vernacular English not with suspicion about their adequacy but from several different perspectives: First, with an appreciation of the natural variation of language—this speaker was, presumably, speaking in exactly the style and with just the grammatical structures that his listeners found appropriate. Second, with an appreciation that such a sentence is equally effective and expressive for its listeners as the revised standard version would be (*Jim and I are going over to his house after school*) if the audience consisted of his teacher. Third, with an understanding that such a sentence does not have "less" grammar than the standard version; it follows common grammatical patterns to the same degree that the standard version does. For instance, in the conversation of many young people, the objective pronoun regularly appears in compound structures *(me and Jim, her and Mary, him and me)* that play the role of sentence subject. Such a pattern is different from Standard English, but it is not random. (It has its own complexity: the speaker would certainly use the subjective pronoun if it stood alone—*I'm going over to Jim's house*—but uses the objective pronoun in compounds.) Fourth, with an understanding that for many people, prejudice against such language may have its roots in prejudice against the people who speak it. Just as Standard English seems "right" because the people who use it are held in high regard, many people view vernacular language as "sloppy" or "uneducated" because that is how they view many of the people who speak that way. A vicious cycle is created. Prejudice about certain people leads to prejudice about their language, which deepens the prejudice about people. Certain features of vernacular English (subject pronouns in the objective case, the omission of certain prepositions, the double negative, an irregular verb form, as in *I seen it*) come to be considered "bad English" because the people who use them are looked down on by others. Then, in turn, other people may be looked down on when their speech includes those stigmatized features. This is what Goal C means by "language-based prejudice."

Goal C encourages the view that knowing grammar can foster an appreciation of *all* language varieties. When students have grammar as a tool for discussing the basic parts of any language, you can help them acquire a broad and democratic understanding of language variation. You can show them that they use different grammatical structures when they talk with their friends *(me and Jim)* compared to when they talk with their teachers *(Jim and I)*. You can encourage them not to look down on or make fun of the ways other people talk by showing them how language that often sounds "wrong" or "weird" usually follows a pattern of its own that is just as consistent as the usage in mainstream English. We will look at lots of examples in the next chapter.

How well do your grammar lessons help students meet these three grammar goals? Ask yourself the following questions about your grammar lesson plans:

- Are students applying grammar to a real communication context?

- Does the lesson take audience and purpose into consideration?
- Will the lesson broaden the students' understanding of and respect for different varieties of English? Different languages?
- Are students using grammatical terminology correctly?

2 Discovering Grammar

Perhaps the purpose of introducing students to grammar—whether in the third grade or at the college level—is to help them discover that all language *has* grammar. For it is not obvious that all languages share a few basic patterns (such as the division of sentences into subjects and predicates) any more than other underlying patterns in our world (such as the cells that compose all living things) are obvious. This chapter discusses new approaches for grammatical consciousness-raising, ways to open students' minds to both the variety and the unity of grammar. The discussion relates to Goal A, helping students communicate comfortably in Standard English and be aware of when to do so, and Goal C, the appreciation of language varieties.

Discovering Grammar through Language Variety

The varieties of English offer you a powerful entranceway through which you can encourage students to discover the structure of language. In particular, the language of ordinary conversation itself provides an essential grammar resource for the classroom.

But an introductory word is in order. You may find that the thought of using ordinary student conversation as a serious grammar resource makes you uncomfortable. After all, much of that conversation is not "correct" English, especially when it is written down on paper or up on a chalkboard and we can see how different it looks from Standard English. It is all well and good to believe that, as the linguists tell you, different language varieties are all "created equal" grammatically. But it is a different matter altogether to confront language use in your own backyard. Your own school and community have their own language issues: the recognizable accents, the regional phrases, the other languages besides English, together with the people's strong opinions about these topics. You as a local English teacher are right in the middle of your community's language issues. You may feel passionately that for the short time your students are in your classroom, you want to help them practice the language they will need to succeed in the adult world and in the world beyond their neighborhood, and you want to do all you can to discourage them from using language that might mark them for failure or discrimination. So part of your success as a teacher, you may feel, is helping your students recognize "bad" or "wrong" language when they see it or hear it.

But consider this: it is not language itself that is the crucial issue here; it is people, and the match between the language they use and the circumstances they find themselves in. Language is "correct" or "incorrect" depending on the circumstances. For adults as well as children, speaking in formal Edited Written English when you are joking around with your family is as out of place as writing a job application that includes instant messaging abbreviations. When you feel the urge to tell a student, or to mark on a paper, that his or her language is "wrong," think to yourself, "'Wrong' for what? 'Inappropriate' for what circumstances?" Remind yourself that the simplistic and absolute judgment that a piece of language is right or wrong can be, at its root, an attempt to judge people. If you can look at the diversity of language in terms of the diversity of people who speak languages as they know and need them, then you and your students can be more open to grammar as a foundation of all language varieties. This chapter will help you move from the "correct/incorrect" view of grammar to a "this is appropriate for this situation/that is appropriate for that situation" approach.

Methodology

Students from elementary through high school may bring to their school writing such home speech patterns as:

My dog name is Bark.

Mom walk me to school yesterday.

I have two brother and two sister.

I might could help you out.

I bought me a new truck.

The car needs washed.

I tried to call youse last night.

I seen the new monster movie already.

Mary be happy.

When a child produces a sentence such as "My dog name is Bark," it can be difficult to resist thinking that the child "lacks possession" or "has left off possession." Such a description, however, is actually a misdiagnosis. The students are not having problems with possession; they are not mistakenly omitting the *'s*. Instead, they have successfully followed the rules for producing possession in their home-speech language variety. That is, in this variety, African American English, possession is shown by adjacency: the possessor occurs next to the thing possessed (possessor:possessed). *My dog name* is not a mistake in Standard English; it follows the grammatical rules of the home speech.

Building on the students' intuitive knowledge of the home language patterns, you can then *add* another language variety to the students' linguistic toolbox. In class discussion, you and the students can contrast the patterns of home speech to the patterns of school speech. Through the contrastive approach, students build an explicit knowledge of the grammar of both language varieties. In the lower grades, teachers might make sentence strips for the classroom walls showing the contrastive patterns of home speech and school speech. During the editing phase of the writing process, the teacher might summarize: "In home speech, you show possession by saying who owns something and then saying the thing they own. In school speech, you also add the 's to the word for the owner." In doing so, you introduce the students to "code-switching," the technique of choosing between language varieties depending on the time, place, audience, and communicative purpose.

Conversational patterns offer constant opportunities for such grammatical discovery and increased grammatical mastery. The same kind of evenhanded analysis you can bring to contrasting the different rules for showing possession applies equally to other language differences. So, for example, when students write *Mary be happy*, the teacher may call on the students to translate the sentence into the Standard English *Mary is usually happy*. Students discover that in African American English, *Mary be happy* means that Mary is generally happy. (This use of the uninflected *be* is called the "habitual *be*.") As they pursue the contrast between habitual action and action in the moment, students may discover that in Standard English, *Mary is happy* can mean either that Mary is happy at the moment or that Mary is generally happy. In contrast, in AAE, *Mary happy*, without the *be*, means that Mary is happy at the moment. (Other differences in the verb systems of AAE and Standard English are described on page 94.)

Another point of contrast is the second-person pronoun *you*. Standard English shows no distinction between the singular and the plural in the second person. Standard English requires us to use *you* regardless of whether we are addressing a whole group or just an individual within that group, an inconvenience that we learn to adjust to. (Think of the ways in which you make your meaning clear when you use *you* in talking to a classroom full of students: "Sam, will you read the answer?" "All of you passed the test." Without *Sam* and *All of*, your students wouldn't know if your *you* referred to all of them, some of them, or one of them.) But students can help supply some of the various inventions of a second-person plural pronoun in home speech, such as *youse, y'all, you'uns,* and *yinz*. These forms show how language communities have been able to preserve a distinction between singular and plural that the standard variety has lost.

Other examples can be discussed in similar contrastive ways. For the sentence "Mom walk me to school yesterday," you might observe that this home speech signals past time through adverbials in the sentence *(yesterday)*, while school speech signals past tense on the verb itself (the *-ed* ending on *walked*). For "I have two brother and two sister," you can explain how African American English signals plurality through number words *(two)* and school speech signals it through the addition of *-s* to the plural noun *(brothers* and *sisters)*. In cases such as "I seen the new monster movie already," you can point out that the different varieties of English have developed different sets of irregular verb forms over time. Here the irregular verb is *seen*. In Standard English, the irregular verb would be *saw*. Neither language variety uses the regular *-ed* form, *seed*, although young children sometimes do so.

Some more examples: When a child brings multiple negation to school, you may be tempted to suggest that the child is speaking incorrectly and illogically. Contemporary Standard English requires single negation and excludes multiple negatives. But this convention is the result of the historical development of English and has nothing to do with logic ("the double negative is wrong because two negatives make a positive"). In Chaucer's time, multiple negation was quite common ("He never yet no villainy not said . . ."). Today, a number of languages include double negatives. In the French *Je ne sais pas*, "I don't know," the two negatives, *ne* and *pas*, are both required. Spanish also uses two negatives—*Yo no se nada*—and as a result the dialect of Hispanic English does too: *I don have no money; I no want nothin*.

Finally, even such simple matters as sentence fragments can become the subject of code-switching and discovery learning. As students describe the structure of conversation (e.g., Q: "Where ya going?" A: "To the store."), they notice that "incomplete sentences" occur as a natural and regular part of casual conversation. If you prompt students for the Standard English "translation," students discover that in contrast to conversation, writing requires the pattern of syntactically complete subject-predicate structures (with some exceptions such as interjections– "Wow!"—and stylistic fragments). After such a lesson, on seeing so-called fragments in the students' writing, you can ask the students to code-switch from the patterns of speech to the expected patterns of writing.

Through such contrasts, students discover that even though other language varieties may be organized differently than Standard English, they are just as organized in their own ways and that Standard English is not the only variety that is grammatical. Of course, while all language varieties are regular and rule-governed systems, we know that certain varieties are privileged over others in the worlds of business and academia. Accordingly, it is the mission of our school system to teach mastery of both spoken and written Standard English in the appropriate contexts. The important news for teachers is that linguistic research is showing increasingly that the most effective way to achieve this mission lies through the techniques of contrastive analysis and code-switching.

In order to use the contrastive and code-switching approaches, you may have to educate yourself in the basic grammar of the language varieties in your classroom. The varieties may include a different language such as Spanish, a widely used and studied language variety such as African American English, or the particular speech patterns of the local community. If you know some of the basic grammatical features of the other languages and language varieties besides Standard English that your students speak, you will find it easier to discuss the language differences with students. (See the two very readable one-volume encyclopedias on language and on English by David Crystal listed in "Source and Resources" for information on various languages and on the varieties of English.) In turn, such discussions of contrasts will help students in three important ways: students will flex their understanding of grammatical structure in language generally; they will understand Standard English itself more clearly; and they will better understand why mastering Standard English is a challenge for those who have not grown up with it.

VIGNETTE: *FLOSSIE AND THE FOX*: CODE-SWITCHING BETWEEN THE LANGUAGES OF HOME AND SCHOOL

How does the contrastive approach actually work in the classroom? And can it work with elementary school children? In this vignette, a second-grade teacher uses role-playing to engage students in contrasting English codes. Notice the preparation that has provided the students with the background necessary to carry out the role-playing. What are some games or role-playing exercises that might call for older students to practice code-switching?

Twenty squirmy second graders wiggle on the red carpet as Mrs. Swords takes a seat in the comfy rocking chair before them. It's reading time and the children can choose whichever book they wish to hear that day. *"Flossie and the Fox!" "Flossie and the Fox!"* the children call. Ever since Mrs. Swords brought *Flossie* to class, the children haven't been able to get enough of it. Never before have they experienced a story in which characters speak like they and their mom and dad and friends do at home. By the third time the children heard the story, they broke into a choral response at one particular point: "Shucks! You aine no fox. You a rabbit, all the time trying to fool me."

But the fox walks a different verbal path. In reply, he tells Flossie, "'Me! A rabbit!' He shouted. 'I have you know that my reputation precedes me. I am the third generation of foxes who have outsmarted and outrun Mr. J. W. McCutchin's fine hunting dogs. . . . Rabbit indeed! I am a fox, and you will act accordingly.'"

Soon the children *knew* the book. They absorbed fox-speak and Flossie-speak.

Now Mrs. Swords invites the children to role-play. "Who would like to talk like a fox today?" Hands shoot up all over the passel of second graders. "OK, Devon, you be the fox. And who wants to talk like Flossie?" Mrs. Swords inquires.

In her blue belted pants, with neatly tucked white shirt, Heather jumps up and down, "Me, I do! I do."

"All right, Heather, you play Flossie."

Back and forth, back and forth, Devon and Heather play.

Children in the class keep tabs. They have already learned that language comes in different varieties or styles and that language comes in different degrees of formality, just like our clothing. The children have already made felt boards and cutouts showing informal and formal clothing and have talked about when we dress informally and when we dress formally. And the children have taken the next steps. They have already looked at and discovered patterns in language—the patterns of informal language and the patterns of formal-speak. They have been primed.

Heather, stretching her linguistic abilities, banters with Devon. "My two cats be lyin' in de sun."

Wait a minute.

The class quickly checks the language chart on the classroom wall. Their chart shows how we signal plurality in both informal and

▷

formal English. Heather has stumbled. She has used the formal English pattern (*two cats*—in which plurality is shown by an *-s* on the noun) when she was supposed to be following the informal pattern (*two cat*—in which plurality is shown by the context or number words).

Mike hollers out, "Heather, wait a *minute*! That's not how Flossie would say it! You did fox-speak! Flossie would say 'My two *cat* be lyin' in de sun.'"

Heather stops. Hands on hips, she considers the wall chart. Mike is right! She regroups and recoups. "My two *cat* be lyin' in de sun!" Heather and Devon are back in their roles. Only one more minute till they swap sides.

In this way, the children practice choosing the forms of language appropriate to the time, place, setting, and communicative purpose. They code-switch between the language of the home and the language of the school.

Sometimes in writing a story, in order to develop a character, children choose the language of nurture, the language they learned on their grandma's knee. Other times, formal times, as when the children write up their research on the relative lengths of dinosaur teeth for their math storyboards, they know they'll choose the language of the professional world because they know that other teachers, the principal, and school visitors will see their work.

Throughout their classroom experiences, children learn to masterfully choose their language to fit the setting. And they do so with joy, verve, and command.

—Rebecca S. Wheeler

Discovering Grammar through Authentic Texts

To help students discover grammar, you need to show them that they can discover grammar wherever they find language. Grammar work sheets and grammar textbooks have their place and their purposes, but their limitations are serious. One of these limitations is that work sheets and textbooks reinforce the students' notion that the sole source and authority for grammar comes from a book of rules and definitions. Although we all turn to reference books when we want to check on the acceptability of a word or a type of phrase, the ultimate resources for judgments of the social acceptability of any language are its literature and the way the language is used by influential groups in society. One of your strategies in teaching grammar can be to encourage students, when they ask "Is this word [or phrase] correct?" to think about whether they have seen it written in the literature and other professional writing they read.

Another limitation of grammar work sheets and textbooks is that they usually present sentences in unnatural isolation, when in the real world sentences are rarely found standing by themselves. In conversations, and in texts of all kinds, sentences live in groups.

The lesson for teachers is that we should teach grammar from authentic texts as much as possible. You can use the literature the students are reading, as well as newspapers and other texts, to demonstrate or teach almost any grammar lesson. You can also use the students' own writing to illustrate points of grammar—to illustrate not just errors but effective grammar as well. Here are some lesson ideas that help students become better observers of the grammatical features of texts, including the ones they write.

Creation of Style Guides

Students can study a given text, such as a newspaper, in order to discover its patterns of grammar and usage. They look for its rules regarding the following:

- capitalization
- paragraph length
- organization of information in text
- the writing of numbers in text
- sentence completeness
- sentence length
- sentence styles
- punctuation choices, such as the comma before the *and* in a series or the use of quotation marks or italics for titles
- voice (active versus passive)
- use of contractions and abbreviations
- beginning (or not beginning) a sentence with a coordinating conjunction
- use of sexist or nonsexist language

The "style guide" method is adaptable to all grade levels. Older students can find texts on their own and work individually or with others to write complete stylistic descriptions. They can formulate and explain such conclusions as their belief that a text is formal (e.g., lack of contractions, long sentences) or that language is nonsexist (e.g., absence of *he* to refer to human beings). With young children, you can give them texts in class and ask them to work with partners; they can look, for example, for words with capital letters and then try to describe the groups these words belong to (e.g., words at the beginning of sentences, names). The conclusions and generalizations that students try to formulate in such exercises are valuable experiences in critical thinking.

Comparison/Contrast

There are many opportunities for comparison/contrast activities in grammar instruction. You can ask students to study the grammatical differences between two texts about the same subject. The students could, for example, compare an owner's manual of a car to an advertiser's brochure or an article from a car magazine: What differences do we find in the textual layout? What words do we find in one but not the other? Which has the longest and the shortest sentences, on average? Which has the most conversational types of sentences? The greatest number of stylistic sentence fragments?

When we ask students to write from one genre to another, we require them to compare and contrast grammatical choices. In going from a news article to a personal letter, for example, students need to adapt the language to the genre while keeping the content essentially the same. To make such an activity meaningful in terms of grammar instruction, students would not only write the information in another genre but also would then analyze *why* these changes were appropriate to a given genre. Such an assignment is a good opportunity to discuss the uses of the first-person pronouns *I* and *me* and the second-person pronoun *you* in writing. (See Chapter 6, "Grammar Superstitions.") When are those pronouns needed and appropriate in writing a letter? An essay? A report? The discussion familiarizes students with the terminology about pronouns and encourages them to think carefully about meaning and audience.

Poetry

Because poetry often uses grammatical structures that differ from ordinary speech, it offers opportunities to teach grammar. Students can look for words, phrases, and clauses that are not in the places they're usually found in sentences. They can discuss the poetic value of such placements, listening for how the placement affects emphasis, rhythm, and rhyme. "Whose woods these are I think I know," the opening line of Robert Frost's "Stopping by Woods on a Snowy Evening," offers such an opportunity. If you ask students to experiment with other ways the line might have been written or spoken, they will discover that it is reversed from the normal sentence order: *I think I know whose woods these are.* They should be able to explain the emphasis and surprise expressed in poetic arrangement.

You can ask students how we know that a piece of writing is a poem. What are the words and phrases that sound poetic? In answering, students discern the grammatical characteristics of not only poetic language but conversation as well.

Advertising

The language of advertising is designed to be fast, persuasive, and memorable. Students can search newspaper and magazine ads for examples of various constructions, including phrases ("Like a Rock," "Easy as Dell"), questions ("Do You Yahoo?" "Got Milk?"), imperatives ("Do It"), exclamations ("50% Off!"), and parallelism ("We've never had more. You'll never pay less."). They can also look for different sorts of wordplay, sharpening their sense of both word meaning and word arrangement: variations on familiar phrases ("This is Cloud Ten. Ford Expedition"), rhymes ("Power Hours"), graphic devices ("choLESS-terol").

Everyday Genres

Ask students to observe the consistent grammatical features of a variety of ordinary genres: the imperative in recipes and instruction manuals (*Rinse chicken; pat dry with paper towels. Twist wing tips under back. If desired, brush with oil*); participles in menus (*seared ahi served with baby carrots drenched in butter*) and greeting cards (*Wishing you well . . . Hoping you feel better soon . . .*); and passive verbs in park brochures (*the rock paintings were discovered by settlers in the 1850s; . . . They were probably created by Native Americans for religious ceremonies*).

Postmortems of Student Writing

Select student-written sentences to share with the class. The sentences might be examples of smooth style, confusing writing, humor, beautiful description, ordinary error, effective punctuation—anything to raise student awareness of sentences, to engage them in a discussion of language, and to use grammatical terminology. You will be surprised by how, if you give students a chance to ponder just about any individual sentence, they can't resist coming up with ways it could or should be changed.

VIGNETTE: HELPING HIGH SCHOOL JUNIORS GET COMFORTABLE WITH SHAKESPEARE'S ENGLISH

Shakespeare's plays may seem to be unlikely material for the study of grammar. But, ideally, grammar instruction is a tool for raising students' awareness of the great diversity of language, including early modern English. Notice how carefully this high school teacher picks and chooses when to employ the technical vocabulary of grammar and when to simplify matters. Notice also how he connects the discussion of sentence structure with discussion of meaning and dramatic impact. Think about the works of literature you teach that might lend themselves to discussions of sentence structure and style.

Before tackling Shakespeare's *Macbeth*, Mr. Doniger gives his students an opportunity to play with some of the language and become more comfortable with it. One of these lessons begins with the students and Mr. D. sitting in a circle. Mr. D. randomly distributes index cards to each student; each index card contains one quotation from the play and lists the act, scene, and character speaking the words. One at a time, students are asked to read their cards aloud; then the quotation is discussed, questioned, analyzed, and explained. The lesson continues as students are randomly asked to "act" their quotations to illustrate their meanings. It finishes with them being challenged to speak their lines with emotions or meanings that are not implied by the words (a theatrical technique known as playing against the text). One student, for example, is asked to read the line "To beguile the time, look like the time" as if it meant "I hate you" or "I love you." The objective is to make the students feel more comfortable with the language and familiar with some of the text before they read the play.

In the process of analyzing the quotations, students get some help by looking at the grammar.

> King: What bloody man is that? He can report,
>   As seemeth by his plight, of the revolt
>   The newest state. (1.2.1–3)

Students, after translating the verbal *seemeth*, have some difficulty understanding what exactly the bloody man can report. When Mr. D. shows that the subordinate clause (*As seemeth by his plight*) is a modifier of the core sentence and not part of just the subject *(He)* or just the predicate, the sentence becomes clearer. Mr. D. keeps the technical terminology limited, referring to the subordinate clause as an idea that alters or deepens the meaning of the core sentence (students are usually able to understand the concept of a core sentence better than the notion of a main clause).

Some students try adding the pronoun *it* before *seemeth;* turning the verb phrase into a clause helps them understand it better. Now all they need to know is that Shakespeare, being a poet, sometimes reverses the normal order of phrases or sentence parts for effect. At this point, their only remaining question is the precise meaning of *state.*

> Macbeth: As easy mayst thou the intrenchant air
>   With thy keen sword impress as make me bleed.
>   (5.8.9–10)

The students find this quotation quite mysterious. Their first problem, once Mr. D. helps them get past the *thou* and the *mayst,* is vocabulary. With Shakespeare, usually nouns are the biggest vocabulary problem, but in this instance the adjective *intrenchant* and the verb *impress* (it's not what the students think it is) need explaining. That much is easy. What helps the students most with this sentence, however, is rearranging the grammatical units in a more modern, and less poetical, order. Mr. D. explains that in Shakespeare's day, adjectives were commonly used as adverbs. By changing the adjective *easy* into the modern adverb *easily,* putting the subject up front, and aligning the correlative subordinators *(as . . . as)* more closely, the students translate the sentence: "You can make me bleed as easily as you can put gashes in the air with your sword." Macbeth's sense of invulnerability becomes clearer.

> Macbeth: To be thus is nothing,
>   But to be safely thus. (3.1.47–48)

Once the students understand the idea of *thus* (here Macbeth means, "To be the king is nothing"), the complications begin. First, reminding students about some grammar vocabulary as he goes along, Mr. D. shows the students that the infinitives are intended as subjects in the two clauses and that the clauses are parallel in structure. The main problem arises from the elliptical second clause, which omits the entire predicate. As Mr. D. puts it, the second clause is left unfinished because the rest of it is understood. He then reminds the students that the word *but* suggests opposition. From there, they easily figure out what is missing in the predicate: "is everything." Once they get this idea, they can discuss the dramatic impact of the line more closely.

> *3rd Apparition:*   Macbeth shall never vanquish'd be until
>   Great Birnan wood to high Dunsinane Hill
>   Shall come against him. (4.1.92–94)

Again, there are vocabulary issues to get out of the way first: *Birnan* (the spelling in *The Riverside Shakespeare*) *wood, Dunsinane, vanquish'd*. But here the students are confused also by the poetic word order. Mr. D. shows them that *shall vanquish'd be* is a change in the normal word order. He also explains that the phrase *Shall come against him* comes at the end of the sentence rather than directly after its subject, *Great Birnan wood*. The students move the phrase, and the meaning becomes clearer. There is time left for a short discussion: did Shakespeare save *Shall come against him* for the end of the sentence in order to create greater tension, to make this idea the strongest point of the warning?

—Paul E. Doniger

3 Teaching the Language of Grammar

The previous chapter focused on raising students' awareness of grammar as language structure. It explained two general approaches for helping students discover grammar: contrasting two types of language with the same or similar content and using authentic texts to observe the grammatical aspects of actual written English. This chapter focuses on an aspect of grammar mentioned in the last section but one that is obviously a topic of its own: grammatical terminology. As grammar goal B explains, one goal of teaching grammar is to give students the terminology for naming the words and word groups that make up sentences—in other words, the parts of speech and the language of phrases and clauses.

In some ways, this goal is the most controversial aspect of teaching grammar. Some teachers sorely resent the time they are required to spend teaching grammatical analysis. They don't see any connection between teaching students to identify the parts of speech and preparing them to communicate effectively in the real world. They are even more resentful when standardized tests require them to cover this material and narrow their already limited classroom time. And, worst of all, they report that their students don't like grammar at all.

But for other teachers, the key to teaching grammatical terminology is making the activity meaningful, and the way to make it meaningful is to connect it with student writing and with their reading as well. Knowing grammatical terminology is not an end in itself but a means toward greater awareness of how language and literature work. The high-stakes tests don't make matters any easier, because they often require grammatical knowledge in its rawest form. But teachers do find ways to make the terms of grammar meaningful for students.

The first part of this chapter introduces you to linguistics-based ways of defining the basic parts of speech; the discussion of the parts of speech continues more fully in Chapter 8, "An Overview of Linguistic Grammar." The second part of this chapter introduces classroom approaches for applying and practicing grammatical terminology. If you need some extra clarification about the grammar terms in this section as you read along, check out the grammar glossary at the end of the book.

Form, Frame, and Function

We have long explained to our students that a noun names a person, place, or thing; a verb describes an action; and so forth. Such definitions might serve as starting points, but there are other easier and more accurate ways to identify the word classes: forms, frames, and functions.

Form. We know that a noun is a noun not only because of its meaning but also because we can change its form in certain ways: nearly all nouns can take endings that show plurality and possession. We recognize *dog, dog's,* and *dogs* as nouns both because of meaning and because of the endings, the forms of the word.

Frame. We also know that a word that stands alone after a determiner such as *the, a, my,* or *this* is a noun: *the dog, a dog, my dog, this dog.* The use of word "frames" helps clarify the part of speech in many cases that we might be hesitant about; *rich* and *poor* are usually adjectives, but they are nouns in *The rich and the poor.*

Function. When a word is used in a sentence, it takes on another vital characteristic: its function. Nouns, for example, function commonly as the subjects, direct objects, indirect objects, and subject complements in sentences. But nouns function not only in "nouny"—or nominal—ways; they function adjectivally and adverbially as well. In the phrase *the school cafeteria, school* is a noun (it's a word that has both plural and possessive forms) even as it performs an adjective's job of telling us about the cafeteria. The noun here functions adjectivally.

So you can encourage students to apply four different tests to words in order to understand the word class they belong to. These tests also help students understand the nature of the words and sentences themselves. In classroom practice with authentic texts, you and the students can be flexible with the tests. You may not need all four to identify every word, and some tests work more reliably or clearly in certain cases than others. We outline them here using nouns as examples. You will find a discussion of the forms and functions of other parts of speech in the section on word classes that opens Chapter 8 as well as in the grammar glossary.

1. Meaning: what a word means (*dog* and *school* name things)
2. Form: what a word looks like, the endings that can be added to it (for nouns, the plural *s* and the possessive *'s; dogs, dog's, schools, school's*)
3. Frame: the words that form a setting in which a word or type of word can fit (most nouns can stand alone after *the* and *a/an; the dog, a school*)

4. Function: what a word does in the sentence (nouns function in many ways, including as the sentence subject *[The dog ran home]*, as the direct object *[He brushed the dog]*, and adjectivally *[The store carries dog collars]*.

Beyond individual words and the roles they play, there are phrases and clauses to consider. Phrases and clauses are *forms*—forms of word groups—and they too serve different *functions*. The phrase is defined as a group of words (or single word in some cases) that acts as a unit or building block in a sentence but is not a clause. The term *phrase* is more important in modern linguistic grammar than you may remember it being in traditional grammar, where it was limited to only a few word groups such as prepositional phrases (*by the door, on the door, under the door,* etc.). In current grammar, the phrase is one of the two building blocks (the other is the clause) of the sentence. It is helpful to remember that phrases in linguistic grammar can be very short or very long. Thus, in the sentence *Dogs come in all sizes, dogs* by itself is considered a noun phrase, the subject of the sentence. In the sentence *The big brown dog that lives across the street is very friendly,* the first nine words also form one long noun phrase (with the noun *dog* as the headword), again as the sentence subject.

A clause can be distinguished from a phrase by its subject-predicate structure. The term *clause* in modern linguistic grammar is more consistent with what you may know already from traditional grammar than the term *phrase* is. *Dogs comes in all sizes* is an independent clause. In the sentence *The dog that lives across the street is friendly, that lives across the street* is an adjectival or relative clause in which the pronoun *that* functions as the clause's subject, and *lives across the street* is the predicate. Phrases and clauses are discussed in more detail under Sentence Constituents in Chapter 8.

Last, beyond the phrase and the clause, we have the sentence itself. The sentence is the unit in which all the other grammatical units—words, phrases, and subordinate clauses—play a role. Generally, for linguists the major type of sentence (there are exceptions and minor sentence types) is independent and includes a finite verb, which is a verb that changes to show tense and thus anchors an event to the speaker's time. Thus, *Karen made the call* includes the finite verb *made* that places the event in the speaker's past. *Karen making the call,* although it indicates the same action, does not stand clearly in a time frame; it could be in the past, as in *I was concerned about Karen making the call,* or the present, as in *What we are hearing now is Karen making the call.*

But beyond such generalizations, the sentence is not the straight-forward unit that teachers and textbooks usually tell their students it is. The traditional definition of a sentence as a complete thought is true of many sentences, but it is obviously a problem with a sentence such as *This is it.* What is a complete thought to the student may not sound complete to the teacher, and vice versa. Even a seemingly self-evident sentence such as *The girl left yesterday,* which instantly sounds complete to the teacher who hears the subject and verb, may sound incomplete and puzzling to the child or young adult who wonders who the girl is, where she left from, and when. Finally, since nearly all written texts consist of sentences, we might expect spoken language to consist of sentences as well, but it is certainly not easy and sometimes not even possible for a listener to hear when one sentence ends and another begins during a conversation.

You can engage students at any grade level in these questions by giving them a selection of sentences from advertising, poetry, prose, and conversation and then asking them to create a workable definition of the sentence. This is a useful exercise in thinking skills and in understanding the limits of definitions. Students will find not only exceptions but also different standards of independence and acceptability in different contexts.

Sentences themselves, of course, are countless in number. But the number of sentence *patterns* in English is much smaller. In fact, there are only seven. And the structure of sentences is even simpler than that in the sense that the patterns are really differences just in the types of verbs and the different arrangements of complements that follow them. The sentence subjects that precede the verbs are steady and predictable: they are usually noun phrases, nouns plus modifiers, such as *Eight-year-old Hassan, who was born in Saudi Arabia.* But sentence patterns begin to differ from one another when we come to the verb. Verbs take three forms, each of which is associated with an arrangement of objects or other complements and each of which establishes the connection between the subject and the predicate that forms the basic meaning of the sentence. There are linking verbs, verbs that link the following complement back to the subject: *Eight-year-old Hassan, who was born in Saudi Arabia, is a good student.* There are intransitive verbs, verbs without complements (although they can be modified), verbs that seem to "contain" the action or state of the subject in themselves: *Eight-year-old Hassan, who was born in Saudi Arabia, walked to school.* Finally, there are transitive verbs, verbs followed by objects and other complements, the simplest example of which is the pattern of verb and direct object, as in *Eight-year-old Hassan, who was born in Saudi Arabia, walked his dog.*

You can find examples and detailed discussion of the seven sentence patterns in the Sentence Pattern section of Chapter 8. As tools for helping students see that the arrangements of words within sentences are simpler than they may appear, the patterns can be a useful part of your repertoire for teaching grammar. You might consider as well traditional sentence diagramming, a graphic way to display sentence structure. Sentence diagramming is explained in Chapter 7, along with suggestions for its effective classroom use.

Practicing and Applying the Language of Grammar

Grammar Hunt

A grammar hunt involves finding particular structures in authentic language. On an elementary level, students can go hunting for simple structures such as a noun series *(I need oranges, bananas, and kumquats)* or prepositional phrases *(under the door, on the door, behind the door,* etc.). Older students can look for such structures as parallelism, in which two or more phrases of the same kind are connected for balance and emphasis *(Give me liberty or give me death* [Patrick Henry]; *I see one-third of a nation ill-housed, ill-clad, ill-nourished* [F. D. Roosevelt; examples from Kischner and Wollin 141]). Ask students to try to draw conclusions about why certain structures are used in certain ways: "Why do some sentences begin with prepositional phrases? What effect does parallel phrasing have here? Are we finding more action verbs or more linking verbs *(is, seems)* in the sports article? Why?"

Recipes

Ask students to compose sentences and text with given grammatical structures and combinations. For example: "Write a description of a zoo animal. Use three action verbs (such as *run, eat*), one linking verb *(is, seems)*, one compound sentence *(The snakes are pretty gross, but lots of people were watching them)*, five prepositional phrases *(in the cage, through the hole)*, etc. This method gets the student out of the "simple sentence" rut and raises awareness of grammatical choices.

A variation is to present patterns of various types of sentences and have students supply the content: "Write a sentence with a compound subject, as in *Bill and Ted had a great adventure.* Write a sentence that ends with an adjectival clause, as in *The mouse gobbled the cheese, which had been sitting in the trap for three days and nights.*"

Inventories

As students read, they keep lists of interesting phrases, classified by grammatical form. They note the functions of various types of structures. After reading a sentence such as *Meredith's dog, a silky golden retriever and her faithful companion, slept at her feet,* for example, a student might note that "Appositives are good for fitting a lot of information into a sentence when there isn't much space."

Playing with Meaning

When we think about grammar, we think of the structure of language, but meaning and structure (semantics and syntax) are the two sides of one coin. Without the patterns of grammar, language would be a jumble of words, with no clues to tell a reader or listener how to connect the meanings of the words. Grammar supplies those connections. In discussing almost any grammatical topic, you can talk with your students about meaning:

- We teach that words are certain parts of speech, but it is productive fun to look at how the same word can serve as different parts of speech with different meanings. *Down* is a good example: *down the street* (preposition), *the down side* (adjective), *to down the ball* (verb)—as well as *a down pillow* (actually, a different word, and a noun used adjectivally). Another example is *fly:* what does it mean to a biologist, a baseball player, a tailor, a tent maker, a pilot?

- Many adverbs can move around quite freely in sentences, but meaning changes when they do so. Students can describe the difference—and the ambiguity—between, for example, *I just met her yesterday* and *I met just her yesterday,* between *Happily, he didn't die* and *He didn't die happily.*

- You can give students different sentence types and observe changes in tone and emphasis. They can compare the simple declarative *Petra wrote that graffiti* with the cleft (rearranged) versions *It was Petra who wrote that graffiti* and *What Petra wrote was that graffiti.*

- Compare active sentences with passive sentences (*Janice hit the ball* versus *The ball was hit by Janice*). The differences in tone and focus are a good topic for class discussion: "When the person appears at the end of the passive sentence, do you think it puts more emphasis on her, or less?" Use real texts such as reports and similar official documents to let students discover how the passive voice places things rather than people in the position of sentence subject or topic. Often in such texts, the people involved in an action are left out completely, as in *The decision was announced yesterday.* Then ask students: "Do you think the sentence ought to include who did the action, or isn't it important?" (If you want to read more about how the placement of sentence elements affects readability, Joseph Williams's book *Style: Ten Lessons in Grace and Clarity* is an excellent discussion of sentence arrangement and stylistic effectiveness.)

VIGNETTE: TEACHING THE PASSIVE VOICE

To help students understand sentence structure, some teachers get physical. Here are two ways to dramatize the passive voice. Can you think of others?

I stand at one side of the room and throw my keys on the floor, telling the class to make me a sentence about what I just did and to begin the sentence with my name. I always get "Ms. Van Goor threw her keys on the floor." I smile and write the sentence on the board.

VG: And the subject of the sentence is?

Class: Ms. Van Goor.

VG: Right! And the verb?

Class: Threw.

VG: Right again.

Now I pick up my keys and do the same thing again, but this time I tell them they must begin the sentence with *The keys.* It takes only a few minutes longer for them to get "The keys were thrown on the floor by Ms. Van Goor." I write that sentence on the board also.

VG: And the subject is?

Class: The keys.

VG: Right! And the verb?

Class (This takes longer, several tries, but eventually someone says it): Were thrown.

VG: Right. Now, in the first sentence, was the subject (I underline the subject once) *doing* what the verb (I underline the verb twice) described?

Class: Yes.

VG: Was the subject *active*, doing something?

Class: Yes.

VG: OK, how about the second sentence? Did the subject (I underline it once) *do* what the verb (I underline it twice) described?

Class (much more slowly!): No-o-.

VG: Was the subject *active*, doing something?

Class: No-o-.

VG: Or was the subject *passive*, just sitting there letting something else *do something to it?*

Class (very tentatively): Passive?

VG: Yeah. The subject didn't *do* anything, but somebody or something did something *to* the subject. I don't know why we call the verb "passive"; it's actually the subject that's sitting there passively letting something happen to it, but that's the way it goes. We say *was thrown* is a *passive* verb.

Another day, I use body diagramming. I call three students up to the front of the room and give them three slips of paper. Written on one is *The new outfielder;* on another, *hit;* and on another, *the ball.* Then I tell these three students to arrange themselves so that they make a sentence and that they must somehow interact with one another in so doing. They do fairly obvious things, the subject usually hitting the verb with enough force to bump the verb into the direct object.

Then I call three more students up, keeping the first three in place. These three get *The ball* and *was hit* and *by the new outfielder.* I give them the same instructions. It takes the students a few minutes, but they usually end up with the subject and verb students out front and the prepositional phrase student a step or two behind them, with a hand holding on to the verb. Then, with both groups of three "acting," I ask the class to tell me the real difference in what's going on up there. Someone will eventually get it: that the action goes to the right in one group and to the left in the other. If I then ask them to look only at the verbs in the two sentences and find a difference, someone will eventually notice that the passive verb has two words. And if that class has by then memorized all the *do, be,* and *have* verbs, I'll ask what family the helping verb belongs to and wait until someone recognizes the *be* family.

If time allows, I get other sets of three students up front and ask them to make up their own short sentences with active and passive verbs and rearrange themselves as necessary. We get lots of

▶

laughs—and students find out not only how to shift from one voice to the other but also how such shifts affect the meaning and flow of the sentence and how indispensable the *be* verb and the past participle are.

—Wanda Van Goor

VIGNETTE: TEACHING PRONOUNS WITH LEGOS

It's not easy to help students grasp the relationships between the parts of sentences. Sometimes, though, the frustration leads to inspiration. Here, Amy Benjamin narrates her discovery of LEGOs as a teaching tool, speaking in some paragraphs to us, in others to herself, and in others to her students, always excited. These days, as a teacher of teachers, Mrs. Benjamin brings LEGOs even to her classes for English teachers. In addition to the placement of "red" and "green" pronouns that she discusses here, what else could you demonstrate by using these blocks?

OK, so I'm teaching this ninth-grade Spanish class about pronoun case and I show them the subjective case and the objective case and how the subjective-case pronouns are used as subjects and the objective-case pronouns are used as direct objects and indirect objects and objects of . . . Wait. They don't know what subjects are. OK, so I show them. Now, that means I guess I can assume they don't know what objects are either. . . . Umm, I'm realizing that the students aren't entirely sure what a verb is. I better explain that.

Well, the next thing I know I'm at Wal-Mart hunting through the toy aisles for a set of giant LEGOs. I go home, spread them out on my living room carpet, and start sticking labels on them to color-code the functions: red for subjective, green for objective, white for prepositions, blue for verbs. No, wait, we need two different verb colors—action and linking—and don't forget the auxiliaries. Oh, and we'll need yellow for conjunctions.

(Can everybody see this? Can you see from the back of the room? Great.) Now, this is a sentence. We'll start with a simple sentence and then move on to a compound sentence. If you have a red

▶

pronoun here, it's acting as the subject, and that means that any other pronoun doing the same thing, in the same part of the sentence, is *also* going to be red. Got that? Yes, and the same thing goes for the greens. The objectives. Those go after the verb . . . right. No, no, no. *After* the verb. Well, in that sentence it only *looks* like the green is before a verb because you're looking at the verb later in the sentence, in another clause. Look at each set of subject-verb-objects. It's always a red pronoun before the verb, green ones after. That one? Well, that's green because it's the object of the preposition. The object of the preposition is always going to be green.

Now, here's what you never, never do: You never, never mix these colors, see? If you mix these colors, you could start a fire in the sentence. You never put a red pronoun on the preposition bar. The preposition always takes the green, the objective case. That's why we call it the object of the preposition.

Now don't be thinking that the red pronouns always come first in the sentence. You could have a prepositional phrase coming first in the sentence, like this: I'll just unhook this prepositional phrase and move it over here right in the beginning of the sentence, and now its object is still green. So we have a sentence with a green pronoun near the beginning and a red pronoun, the sentence subject, after that.

Colors and visuals are powerful learning modes. The LEGOs approach allows us to show which parts of the sentence go together and what happens on either side of the verb. The LEGOs help native English speakers see the sentences they speak every day, but they are even more helpful when you are teaching a foreign language. When students are learning a foreign language, they need to know grammatical terminology because their ear is not attuned to the sound of the standards of the new language as it is (albeit imperfectly) to the sound of the standards of English.

The LEGOs approach ought to work with other concepts as well, such as verb endings, suffixes and prefixes, and parts of speech. I'm planning on asking for a LEGOs grant so that students can construct sentences at their seats. I'll let you know how that goes.

—Amy Benjamin

VIGNETTE: TEACHING THE ABSOLUTE PHRASE

This vignette describes a writing exercise for introducing students to a structure that adds details to a sentence in a compact way. The lesson also makes use of an important teaching approach: sentence combining. If you were this teacher, how would you follow up this lesson?

The teacher brings to class a picture of a lone tree on a hill; some leaves on the tree are still green and some have turned orange and red. The teacher asks students to create sentences that describe what they see in the picture, and the teacher then writes the sentences on the board.

Then the teacher asks which of these sentences has the most panoramic view of the tree. After various suggestions, the teacher and class settle on *The tree stands alone on the hill.*

Next the teacher asks the students to choose a sentence on the board that works like a zoom lens that is looking more closely at the tree. The students settle on *The leaves on the tree are turning red and orange.*

"Now," the teacher says, "We will attach this sentence to the first one by dropping the *are.*" The teacher writes on the board, *The tree stands alone on the hill, the leaves on the tree turning red and orange.*

"Does that sound right?"

"No," a student answers, "because we already have *tree* in the sentence. We wouldn't say *leaves on the tree,* but *its leaves.*" So the teacher makes this change: *The tree stands alone on the hill, its leaves turning red and orange.* She explains that *its leaves turning red and orange* is an absolute phrase, a noun phrase plus a modifier following it, relating to the sentence as a whole. The base sentence gives the big picture and the absolute phrase gives details, like a zoom lens.

—Edith Wollin

VIGNETTE: SUBJECT-VERB AGREEMENT: SLICING THE APPLE

Sometimes, showing students how to edit an error is to open Pandora's box. Students at all levels sometimes need to go back over the basics when confronted by a problem with a sentence. The process may feel discouraging to the teacher, but review gradually strengthens students' language awareness. Here, one teacher about to discuss subject-verb agreement has come prepared. What grammar lessons have left you thinking you needed to review the basics?

It is midsemester, and Dr. Krauthamer's English Composition I students have been given their midterm grades. They are progressing well in essay structure, development, and coherence, but grammar, usage, and mechanics are still troubling areas. Dr. K. decides to focus on one grammar topic each week, and this week it is subject-verb agreement. She writes a sentence on the board from one of their midterm essays: *One year the drought got so bad that the water in these tanks were very low.* She asks the class, "What is the problem with this sentence?"

After a while, a student volunteers an answer, "The *were* should be *was.*"

Another student declares, "You can't say 'tanks was.' Isn't that wrong?"

Dr. K. says, "Let's try a little demonstration of subject-verb agreement."

She places an apple, a knife (this is college!), and a cutting board on the desk. Bemused, the students wait for direction. Standing in front of the class, Dr. K. says, "Now watch what happens and then write a single sentence about what you see." Dr. K. then takes the knife, slices the apple on the cutting board, and says to the students, "Okay, write!"

After a few minutes, Dr. K. asks the students to write their sentences on the chalkboard. As they look at the board, she says, "My first question for you is, are these all sentences?" She points to one and reads it aloud: *"A slice of apple on the cutting board."*

"No, that's not a sentence because there's no verb. A sentence must have a verb," says one student.

"Right! Now, how about this one," says Dr. K, pointing to another, *"A teacher cutting an apple with a knife."*

▶

"Yes, it's a sentence because the verb is *cutting,* since it shows an action," says one student. "It also has a subject, which is *teacher.*"

"It still doesn't feel like a sentence," says another. "Something's missing."

"We have to put in a real verb, like *is,*" says one of the students. "It's a sentence if we say, *The teacher is cutting an apple with a knife.*"

"What makes *is* a real verb?" asks Dr. K.

No one responds.

"Let's look at some of the other sentences," says Dr. K. "What are the real verbs here?" She turns to the board and says, "Call out the real verbs, and I will double-underline them." The class recites together, laughing as the occasional wrong word is shouted.

"I don't understand," says one student. "I was taught that verbs indicate actions, and to me *slicing* and *cutting* are actions. Why aren't they verbs?"

"They are verb forms," says Dr. K, "but they aren't the *finite verbs.* They don't show whether they are in the past or the present, and they don't change depending on the subjects. When we talk about subject-verb agreement, we are concerned with the finite verb, the verb that will usually change depending on the subject. Let's look now for the subjects of these sentences, and I will single-underline them." Again the class recites together, and again some students call out the wrong words.

"Now I'm really confused. In *The teacher used the knife to cut the apple,* why isn't the subject *the knife?* Isn't the knife doing the cutting?" asks one student. "I thought the subject is what is doing the action."

"Now we're talking about semantic roles," says Dr. K. "The knife is the instrument—the tool used to perform the action; the teacher is the agent—the entity responsible for the action; the apple is the patient—the entity that receives the action; and this action is cutting. You can write many different sentences about this one semantic situation, and any one of those semantic roles can become the grammatical subject. Let's try it. Write sentences about what you just saw and use different subjects." The students come up with a variety of sentences, including:

The *knife* sliced the apple.

The *teacher* cut the apple.

The *apple* was sliced with the knife.

The *board* is what the apple was sliced on.

Cutting an apple is a messy thing to do in a classroom.

The class is amazed at how many sentences they can create from this one action. "So what do we mean by *subject*?" asks Dr. K.

"It's whatever agrees with the finite verb," says one student.

"Good! Now, here's something to watch out for when you're writing," says Dr. K. "A lot of subject-verb agreement errors happen when the subject and verb are so far apart that we don't always see their connection. Let's compose a sentence in which the subject is separated from the verb."

"*The teacher, trying to keep the students entertained, cuts the apple,*" says one student.

"Good! Can we make it even longer than that?"

"*The teacher, trying to keep the students entertained after a very long day at school and with lots of other problems on their minds, cuts apples in class.*"

"Now let's make the subject plural."

"*The teachers, trying to keep the students entertained after a very long day at school and with lots of other problems on their minds, cut apples in class.*"

Dr. K. points back to the original sentence:

"*One year the drought got so bad that the water in these tanks were very low.* We were wondering whether *were* is the right word. Is it a finite verb? Could it change tense? Could it change to agree with a different subject?"

Most students nod.

"Now take your time with the next question and remember what we were saying about the subject and verb being separated. What is the subject of *were*?"

A couple of confident hands: "*Water.*"

"So what is the problem with this sentence?"

"Subject-verb agreement!"

—Helene Krauthamer

4 Flexing the Students' Sentence Sense

The previous two chapters suggested ways to help make students aware of language structure and ways to help them understand and practice basic grammatical terminology. This chapter focuses on students' innate sense of the sentence and on how students can strengthen that ability and put it to good use. The chapter is related to the grammar goals of writing in Standard English and of understanding how the structure of sentences affects the clarity of texts.

Sentence Boundaries

Often we teach students to identify sentence fragments by checking for a verb, a subject, and completeness of thought. But if you are not familiar with it already, you should also try the very practical approach to such errors described by Rei Noguchi, author of *Grammar and the Teaching of Writing: Limits and Possibilities* and a professor at California State University, Northridge. Noguchi's approach is a simple and effective way to help students find their own basic writing errors. The pragmatic tests he describes draw on the innate sentence sense of native speakers. Noguchi points out, for example, that a group of words is a complete sentence if it makes sense after a frame such as *They refused to believe that.* Neither a run-on sentence nor a fragment will sound right in that context. Take the fragment *Whatever you could do to help my sister. They refused to believe that whatever you could do to help my sister* will not sound sensible or complete to a native English speaker.

Native speakers also have the ability to turn sentences into several types of questions, such as *Isn't it fair?*, *Why isn't it fair?*, and *It isn't fair, is it?* Such questions are useful for a number of purposes, one of which is to help identify run-on sentences. A sentence might not appear at first to the student as two sentences run together, but the error is more visible if the student attempts to turn it into a question. A student might write, for example, *You weren't in class for a whole month, it isn't fair.* If you ask the student to turn the statement into a question, the student could produce either *Weren't you in class for a whole month, it isn't fair?* or *You weren't in class for a whole month, it isn't fair, is it?* You can show the student that in both these versions, part of the sentence is a question but part of it is not, a division that shows there are actually two sentences present. If the student writes *Weren't you in class for a whole month, it isn't fair, is it?*, it is not difficult to show the student that this strange-sounding sentence is actually two questions.

Students should be encouraged not only to correct fragments and run-ons but also to experiment with them. In *Image Grammar*, Harry Noden explains that students can imitate the way professional writers use fragments to emphasize breaks and separation of images. Similarly, students can try their hand at writing extended sentences to create a sense of flow or acceleration or mass. His discussion of long and run-on sentences is especially interesting. As an example from professional writing, Noden quotes a 126-word sentence by the writer Tom Wolfe from *The Right Stuff* that conveys the intense feeling of acceleration in an F-100 fighter jet. Noden then offers a sentence written by Emelia Hiltner, an eighth-grade student, in which she adds multiple phrases and clauses to create the picture of a fire out of control:

> The fire roared, rushing from building to building, devouring everything in its path, destroying and wasting, hot and hungry, quick and powerful, like a starving beast, flames licking towards the sky, as sirens screamed and firemen shot gallons of water, taking away the life of the fire. But they were too late. (98)

According to Noden,

> Meaning takes precedence over rules. Teaching this notion to students can actually strengthen their understanding of conventions, rather than diluting it as some teachers might expect. When teachers help students see conventions as an aid to meaning, struggling students can better recognize when fragments and run-ons don't work, and confident students can better understand why writers break the rules. (98)

VIGNETTE: GRAMMATICAL CHOICES, SENTENCE BOUNDARIES, AND RHETORICAL EFFECTS

Writing sentences on a board and asking students to compare them and choose from them is a surefire way to generate discussion. Students can't resist disagreeing, complaining, and revising. Here, such an exercise leads, as it often does, to important ideas about conventional correctness and sty-

▷

listic options. What points would you like your students to absorb about sentence boundaries, and what are some "choice" exercises that might help them get there?

Tim Reilly begins his Monday ninth-grade English class like this: "I'm gonna tell you a story. Actually, three stories. Here they are." Tim writes on the board:

1. The shark bit his leg to the bone.

2. To the bone, the shark bit his leg.

3. The shark bit his leg. To the bone.

"Now. Are these three stories the same?"

"Yeah," says Nate. "The same thing happens. Just the words is different."

"What words are different?" Tim asks.

Nate pauses, looking at the three sentences. Tim can see him mentally counting and comparing the words. "Well, the words is the same, but they in a different place. It mean the same."

"Which of these stories do you think is the most violent?"

The kids start calling out, eager to give their opinions on the rhetorical effects of phrase and clause placement, though they are not using these terms. After some consideration and debate, most agree that version 3 is the most violent, the most dramatic.

"It's because first you hear that a shark did some biting on the guy's leg. Then after you got that, you hear it's down to the bone. That makes it more harsh-like," Ali says.

"But that ain't a sentence," Paul insists. "You can't say that in a story."

"Why can't you?" Tim asks.

Paul looks surprised. "You gotta write in complete sentences."

"But tell me: if you're writing a story and you want the story to be exciting and dramatic and violent and graphic, and writing a phrase as a sentence will do that for you, why would you not go for it?"

The kids protest that the rules have always been that anything they write for their English teacher has to be in complete sentences. Even in social studies and science, their teachers want complete sentences.

"We get points off if we don't have a sentence," Jaime says.

"Have you ever seen stand-alone phrases in a story?" Tim asks, aware that he's used an unfamiliar term and hoping that the students will figure it out in context.

"A what?" Kevin asks.

"A stand-alone phrase," Tim repeats. "What do you think that means?"

"That's like a phrase that thinks it's a sentence. Like *to the bone*."

Tim nods. "Look for stand-alone phrases in your novel." The class is reading *The Old Man and the Sea*. He waits for them to find stylistic fragments. They find several, including:

> "Then he said aloud, 'I wish I had the boy. To help me and to see this.'"

"That's a thought," Tim explains. "Thoughts don't have to be written in complete sentences. Neither do the things we say. The dialogue. And if we want to emphasize something in a story, to make it more dramatic, we can write it as a stand-alone phrase. Some people call that a stylistic fragment. It's a piece of a sentence that the writer wants to stand alone for some reason."

"So how are we supposed to do it?" Kristen wants to know.

"You're supposed to do what your readers expect, so they will know what you mean. Usually, that means complete sentences, but not always. You can write a stylistic fragment if you have a good reason. One good reason is to make your words sound natural."

Some of Tim's students get it; some aren't ready to make fine distinctions in their written language. Tim's lesson about stylistic fragments isn't over. He will build on the shark story to teach emphasis, word order, and voice. Tim's instruction in the subtleties of grammatical choices and how they affect meaning will be ongoing and informed by literature and real language.

—Amy Benjamin

Sentence Flexibility

Inexperienced writers find it difficult to make changes in the sentences they have written. Expanding sentences, rearranging the parts of a sentence, combining sentences—these skills do not come easily. So any exercises that help students acquire sentence flexibility have value. Although the following methods do not require the students to know grammatical terminology, your class discussions of sentence arrangement will remain limited and awkward unless the students can name the basic sentence parts.

Sentence Combining

Sentence combining is a tested method for improving the maturity of student writing. Beginning with the work of Kellogg Hunt, Frank O'Hare, William Strong, and others in the 1960s and 1970s, studies have shown that sentence-combining exercises are effective in building certain writing skills. Students progress from simple exercises in insertion and combining in the early grades toward exercises in embedding one clause in another (Strong). Doing so involves making decisions about conjunctions such as *and* and *but*; relative pronouns such as *who, that,* and *which*; punctuation; and ellipsis (the omission of words). Practice in manipulating word groups within and between sentences helps the revising process become gradually more automatic for writers of all ages. They learn to hear and hold sentences in their heads more easily as they revise. As a result, they struggle less to find sentence structures that express their ideas. Several good books with sentence-combining exercises are available; see the works in "Sources and Resources" by Killgallon; Kischner and Wollin; Morenberg and Sommers; and Strong.

Sentence Imitation

While sentence combining is a technique that students need some time and practice to get the hang of, sentence imitation can be used more easily and spontaneously because—well, it's imitation. Give your students a model sentence and ask them to write one like it. Depending on your purpose, the sentence could be an example of a grammatical structure you are teaching, a type of sentence (such as a dramatically short one), or simply one that is admirable in some way. Students write their version of the sentence, imitating its key features. They then go on to include examples of the model pattern in their papers. This practice integrates reading skill, stylistic experimentation, and grammatical understanding.

Code-Switching

The term *code-switching* is often applied to the differences in the way people speak depending on the context of their conversation (see Chapter 2), but it is a useful concept for working on sentence flexibility as well. Ask students to write the same assignment in different ways in order to adapt to different audiences and purposes: "Suppose you were in a minor car accident. Write out how you would describe it to your friends, your parents, a police officer." Students should explore differences in word choice, tone, and sentence structure.

VIGNETTE: SENTENCE IMITATION

This teacher employs a grammar/writing instructional strategy that has ancient roots: having students imitate the sentences of well-known writers. The teacher selects a model sentence that is both a striking one in the literary work and one whose pattern will be new but manageable to student writers. Notice the teacher's flexibility about some of the details in the model sentence and the options for students implicit in the direction to use a similar sentence anywhere in their next paper. Look over the literature that you teach for sentences that might serve as models for imitation.

Mr. Held's English class has been discussing Alice Walker's story "Everyday Use." Now, toward the end of class, it's time to make one addition to their next writing assignment: the students will be writing a sentence modeled on a sentence from the story.

"Let's go back to the start of the story and look at Walker's writing style. Isaiah, would you read the opening paragraph? Loud and slow."

Isaiah clears his throat and sits forward. "'I will wait for her in the yard that Maggie and I made so clean and wavy yesterday afternoon. A yard like this is more comfortable than most people know. It is not just a yard. It is like an extended living room. When the hard clay is swept clean as a floor and the fine sand around the edges lined with tiny irregular grooves, anyone can come and sit and look up into the elm tree and wait for the breezes that never come inside the house.'"

"Thank you. Take a minute to look at the sentences. What do you notice about any of them?

Austin asks, "What are the 'grooves'"?

Mr. Held takes him back to the sentence. "Yes, that's a little puzzling. Austin, read the full sentence again, out loud."

Austin reads, "'When the hard clay is swept clean as a floor and the fine sand around the edges lined with tiny irregular grooves,

▶

anyone can come and sit and look up into the elm tree and wait for the breezes that never come inside the house.' Okay, there's sand around the clay part of the yard and they rake it or something so that it's wavy. I think I've seen that kind of thing."

"Okay. Other comments on the sentences or the writing style here, just in this paragraph?"

"It's very descriptive," Anjali says.

"Explain, please."

"Well, that long sentence tells you a lot about the clay yard and how everyone can sit there and enjoy the breeze. It's cooler than being in the house. Shouldn't there be an *is* after *edges*? It should be 'the fine sand around the edges *is* lined with tiny irregular grooves,' shouldn't it? It sounds funny."

"You can leave out the verb when you have already used the same verb before it and this is a second phrase with the same pattern. It's like writing, *My shoes are black, my shirt, yellow.*"

Mr. Held continues. "Let's look at the core of the sentence, which comes after the opening clause that starts with *When.* We go through the two *when* things that happen and then we come to the sentence subject, which is *anyone.* What is the verb that goes with *anyone?* What does *anyone* do?"

"*Come.* Anyone can come."

"Okay. Right."

"What about *sit?*"

"Okay. That too."

"*Look up.* Isn't that a verb here?

"Yes it is. That's three verbs for *anyone.* 'Anyone can come and sit and look up.' Is that it?"

"*Wait.*"

"Good. Four verbs. This is the basic pattern of the sentence I want you to try to imitate for your next paper. I'll put it on the board. It starts with *when.* It goes like this: When something is or does something and something is something—you can put in the second *is,* and you can use a different verb if you want—then a person can this and this and this and this. That's four verbs. Notice that after the third and fourth verbs there are some descriptive words, and you can try to work some into your sentence. Let's practice. Try writing out a sentence like this, following this pattern on the board, about anything."

Mr. Held gives the students a few minutes, until he sees that most of them have written something. "What do you have?"

"When I get up early and it's still dark out, I yawn and drag myself around and force myself to eat breakfast and get to school."

"When my friend Dave comes over and we play video games, we can sit there for hours and play the game and talk about it and compete with each other."

"When my mother gets home from work and takes off her coat, she smiles and kisses me and sits down and starts to talk about her day."

As these three examples show, students can usually find content that fits well with the particular grammatical characteristics of a model sentence the teacher gives them. The process makes them conscious of sentence structure and gives them the satisfying experience of using a sentence pattern they might not have written otherwise.

—Brock Haussamen

The Rhetoric of the Sentence

Grammatical choices have rhetorical effects. *Rhetoric* refers to the way we arrange language to have the desired effect on our readers or listeners. We organize our sentences differently depending on who our audience is, what we want to emphasize, and how we want to sound. Sentences work together with other sentences to form paragraphs, poems, and conversations that we hope communicate effectively. You can introduce your students to these links between sentence structure and the effectiveness of language. In this section, we discuss a couple of topics in this area, but be aware that it is a large one, and Martha Kolln's *Rhetorical Grammar: Grammatical Choices and Rhetorical Effects* and Joseph Williams's *Style: Ten Lessons in Clarity and Grace* can tell you much more.

Traditional grammar defines *subject* and *predicate* as the topic of the sentence and what is being said about it, respectively, and then leaves them at that. But the terms are more than just two more words in the list of ways sentences can be divided up. If the sentence is the unit of a language that expresses an idea, then the subject-predicate structure is the arrangement that makes this expression possible. When people make meaning, they make predicates about subjects.

Using examples from literature, from newspapers, and from their own papers, students can learn to look at all kinds of sentences as the selection of a topic (in most sentences, the subject) and the making of a comment about it (the predicate). By observing this pattern, they can see the repetition of the subject/topic across sentences, a progression that gives a paragraph its cohesion. In the following example, the grammatical subjects are underlined and the complete predicates are italicized.

> *Not for the first time,* <u>an argument</u> *had broken out over breakfast at number four, Privet Drive.* <u>Mr. Vernon Dursley</u> *had been woken in the early hours of the morning by a loud, hooting noise from his nephew Harry's room.*
>
> *"Third time this week!"* <u>he</u> *roared across the table. "If you can't control that owl,* <u>it</u>*'ll have to go!"*
>
> <u>Harry</u> *tried, yet again, to explain.*
>
> *"*<u>She</u>*'s bored," <u>he</u> said. "<u>She</u>'s used to flying around outside."* (The opening of *Harry Potter and the Chamber of Secrets*, J. K. Rowling, Scholastic Press, 1999)

Ask students to make a list of the sentence subjects in a paragraph. Then show them that those subjects are the topic under discussion. They are what the paragraph is about; if the sentence subjects are too different from one another, then the paragraph is confusing. In the example here, the discussion focuses on the argument between Harry and his uncle about the owl. (Students might notice as well that Mr. Dursley refers to the owl quite impersonally as *it*, while Harry uses *she*.)

Another rhetorical pattern that is profoundly important is the distinction between familiar information and new information within the sentence. Its basic principle is that in most (not all) sentences the information early in the sentence, including the sentence subject itself, is known or familiar to the reader who has read the previous sentences; the material in the predicate, the sentence's comment on the subject or topic, is new. The known-new pattern adds a new dimension to such grammar topics as pronouns (which are usually links to known information in that the pronoun refers back to something or someone), transitional expressions, and careful selection of a sentence's grammatical subject.

The excerpt from *Harry Potter and the Chamber of Secrets* shows this pattern in both straightforward and subtle ways. At the end, the pronouns *he* and *she* present familiar information, since the reader knows their antecedents. More subtly, "Mr. Vernon Dursley," at the start of the second sentence, is not exactly familiar information (this is the opening of the book), but it is information that the reader is prepared for because the previous sentence ends with the reference to the address at "number four, Privet Drive."

The known-new pattern coincides with another important rhetorical feature of sentences: the tendency for the vital information to fall toward the end of the sentence, a tendency known as *end focus.* The new information toward the end of the sentence naturally receives the most attention. In speech, the speaker usually gives it the most stress. In contrast, as the examples from *Chamber of Secrets* show, the subject is generally known information; in fact, it's often a pronoun.

Writers and speakers have options for varying the arrangement of sentences in order to place the new or important information where it will receive the proper attention. One option is the passive voice. Let's look again at the second sentence from the *Chamber of Secrets* excerpt, a sentence in the passive voice:

> Mr. Vernon Dursley had been woken in the early hours of the morning by a loud, hooting noise from his nephew Harry's room.

If this sentence had been written in the active voice, with the hooting noise as the sentence subject and the waking as an activity rather than an effect, the first three sentences would look like this:

> Not for the first time, an argument had broken out over breakfast at number four, Privet Drive. A loud, hooting noise from his nephew Harry's room had woken Mr. Vernon Dursley in the early hours of the morning.
> "Third time this week!" he roared across the table.

For the reader just opening the book and starting to read, this second sentence, with its opening reference to the hooting noise, would probably seem startling. The noise seems unconnected to the known information about the breakfast argument in the previous sentence. By comparison, the original version opens with Mr. Dursley, a party to the argument, and then settles in to focus on the loud noise that is the topic of discussion for the next few sentences. The passive voice allows the information in the sentence to fall in the most effective order.

In addition to the passive voice, we use other common devices to organize our sentences so that the emphasis falls where we want it to. One of them is known as the cleft structure, so called because the sentence is cleaved or divided and rearranged. The *it*-cleft begins with *it* and places the stress on the word or phrase that comes a couple of words later. We often use the *it*-cleft spontaneously. Instead of saying, "They finally showed up at four o'clock," we might say, for emphasis, "It was four o'clock when they finally showed up." The *what*-cleft is also common: "What I liked best about the dinner was the dessert" (instead of "I liked the dessert best").

In addition to cleft sentences, the use of the expletive *there* (*expletive* means it has no meaning but is only filling a place in the sentence structure) can also help the writer put the stress where she or he wants it. The *there*-transformation, as it is called, does not usually rearrange a sentence to the same degree that a cleft-transformation does, but it delays the sentence subject for a couple of words, putting it after the verb *to be,* giving it greater focus. In "Letter from Birmingham Jail," for example, Martin Luther King Jr. might have written, *Of course, nothing about this kind of civil disobedience is new;* instead he wrote, *Of course, there is nothing new about this kind of civil disobedience.* The *there* version focuses our attention strongly on *nothing new.*

These notions of using the passive voice and using *its* and *theres* to open sentences may sound controversial to you. It's possible that you, as well as our students, have been told to avoid the passive voice and not to start sentences with empty *its* and *theres.* These are grammar myths. Although young students learning to write may overuse such techniques at times, it's also true that skilled writers—and all of us when we are speaking—use them to control emphasis, to manipulate and vary the pattern of known and new information.

VIGNETTE: TEACHING ENGLISH LANGUAGE LEARNERS THE KNOWN-NEW PATTERN

Most sentences move from familiar information to new information. And the familiar or given information in a sentence was new information in an earlier sentence, usually in its predicate. (In Arthur Miller's Death of a Salesman, *for example, Linda says to Willy, "But you didn't rest your mind. Your mind is overactive, and the mind is what counts, dear."* Mind *becomes the familiar or known information in the second sentence after being introduced in the predicate of the first sentence.) This pattern of flow and connection is neglected in the teaching of grammar, and that's a shame because it has many uses. Here, Amy Benjamin uses it to help an English language learner. What are other English lessons in which it might be valuable?*

In teaching English language learners how to retell stories, I've found the known-new principle extremely helpful. Here's how we do it: Let's say that my ninth-grade student Thalita knows a story. It could be a story that her class has read, or a movie, or something she's seen on television. I want her to advance her English skills by retelling, or summarizing, the story using the known-new principle of textual cohesion to guide her from one sentence to the next. I give Thalita a graphic organizer that looks like this:

Sentence 1:_____/_____

Sentence 2:_____/_____

Sentence 3:_____/_____

Sentence 4:_____/_____

Sentence 5:_____/_____

Thalita and I will use the organizer to set up the textual feed from the predicate of each sentence, after the slash mark, to the following sentence.

> *Me:* Tell me about Romeo and Juliet.
>
> *Thalita:* I don't understand the words.
>
> *Me:* I know the words are hard. Just tell me: Who are Romeo and Juliet?
>
> *Thalita:* Boyfriend and girlfriend.
>
> *Me:* Are they young or old?
>
> *Thalita:* Young.
>
> *Me:* Romeo and Juliet are young lovers. That's your first sentence. *Lovers* is another word for "boyfriend and girlfriend."

After Thalita writes this for sentence 1, I need to transition her into sentence 2, advancing this information. I ask her to circle *young lovers.*

I say, "Now let's say something about Romeo and Juliet, the young lovers. Let's start the next sentence with 'They.' 'They . . . ' Tell me something about them."

She says, "They have problem."

I explain that we use *a* if there is one problem. If there are many problems, then we don't use *a.*

"There is many."

"Just add *s* to show many."

"They have problems." She writes the sentence down and then I ask her to circle *problems.*

"Now you can talk about their problems. Start with one of their problems. You can start your next sentence with 'A problem' or 'One of their problems' and then say what the problem is."

▶

"A problem is their parents."

"Good. Now you can talk about their parents."

"Is OK?"

"Is what OK?"

"Is OK you have 'problems' and 'problems' in the next?"

"That's fine. It shows you are still talking about the same thing. Every new sentence needs to say something more about the sentence you just finished."

Thalita writes: "They are parents do not like they lovers. They are fight."

Obviously, Thalita is not ready for grammatical terms such as *subject, predicate, referent,* and *pronoun.* But I need to have these terms and categories in my head if I am to be midwife to Thalita's emergent English language skills. For now, I'll keep these terms invisible to her, coaxing one sentence out of another as we go along.

Here are some prompts that help Thalita get from one sentence to the next:

- "Here's another way to say this."

- "We can take this group of words and call them 'it' or 'this' in the next sentence."

- "What do they do next?" (This prompts an action verb.)

- "Now we can call these words _____." (This prompts a synonym or collective noun.)

- Once Thalita has a cohesive sequence of simple sentences, we can add detail through adjectives, adverbs, and prepositional phrases.

    + To prompt adjectives, I ask, "What kind?" "What does it look like?"

    + To prompt adverbs, I ask, "When?" "How?"

    + To prompt prepositional phrases, I ask, "When?" "Where?"

Thalita's placement in a mainstream ninth-grade classroom where students are reading a Shakespearean play may seem overwhelming to her and to me. But relying on the known-new pattern helps her understand the basics of the story and advances her English language skills. As Friar Lawrence advises: "Wisely and slow. They stumble that run fast."

—Amy Benjamin

5 Non-Native Speakers in the English Classroom

It's difficult enough trying to strengthen the language skills of students who have spoken English all their lives. The suggestions in this book have made sense to you, perhaps, and have opened up some new possibilities for teaching grammar to students who have been chattering away in English for years. But what about your students who are still trying to learn English? These students range from those who enter our schools with no English at all to those whose speech is proficient but whose writing lacks the fluency of a native speaker's. Some of these students may be able to read and write in their own language, but many cannot. Unless you have been trained in TESL (teaching English as a second language), you probably don't know much about how to address the needs of these students. You may not be sure at all if direct instruction in English grammar will be helpful to them, or if it is, how to go about it, or if you knew how to go about it, how to find the time to focus on what seem to be unusual English problems.

This chapter considers four questions. At the end, you will find a list of sources that address the topics more fully.

1. What do you need to know about your ESL students?
2. How are other languages different from English?
3. What general strategies are helpful with ESL students?
4. What are some specific ways you can help?

What Do You Need to Know about Your ESL Students?

To work with students who are learning the English language, you first need to consider some questions about them that pertain to the rudiments of second language learning:

1. *How closely is the student's native language related to English?* English is a Germanic language with Latinate and Greek influences. It is cousin to the Romance languages: Spanish, Portuguese, French, Italian, and Romanian. The ESL student whose native tongue is a Romance language will find many cognates (related, similar words, such as *library* in English and *el libro*, "book," in Spanish) that open doors to English words. On the other hand, East Asian languages (as well as African and Na-

tive American languages, among others) have much less common ground in terms of sentence structure, word order, formation of plurals, and the sounds themselves. For most of our students from Asia, their native languages have very few English cognates for them to hang their hats on.

2. *What is the student's functional level as a speaker of English?* In the best of circumstances, your school will have an ESL specialist who will evaluate the English proficiency of your students and give you an accurate report.

3. *How old is the student?* Psycholinguistic research indicates that the older one is, the harder it is to assimilate a new language. Before puberty, language is learned intuitively, in the left hemisphere of the brain. After puberty, we lose the ability to learn language intuitively, and language learning becomes a right hemisphere function, more difficult to keep in long-term memory.

4. *Is the student socializing with English speakers?* Anything you can do to encourage socialization in English would be helpful. If you've ever been in a country where you don't speak the language, you know how lonely and frustrating it can feel. Schools that care about their ESL students arrange for social opportunities such as clubs, buddy systems, breakfasts, and invitations to events. They see to it that their community welcomes newcomers, has a place for them. Teachers who care about their ESL students express an active interest in their cultures and languages, offering opportunities for them to communicate and make friends and making sure everyone in the class knows how to pronounce their names—in general, presiding over an atmosphere of invitation and inclusion.

5. *Can the student read and write in his or her own language? How well?* Students will learn the conventions of writing in English more easily if they have basic writing skills in their home language. But don't assume this is the case, even for older students.

6. *Is the student happy to be here?* Affective factors play an important role in second language learning. Aversion to a culture, not wanting to be here, and longing for home and family can impede learning English. These students need adults in the school to look after them. Sad to say, sometimes our ESL students are exploited as laborers and not given time and opportunity to study.

The first and best way to differentiate instruction for your ESL students is to be a gracious host to them in your classroom. The other students will follow your example. Help the ESL students feel they are part of the classroom, that they have much to share about their culture and language, and that you and the other students look forward to learning from them. Don't just say all this to sound polite. Create authentic opportunities in which the students can actively contribute their unique knowledge and points of view; you will find suggestions on the pages that follow.

Finally, a word about the word *foreign*. If you lived in a place and went to school there, would you want to be considered a foreigner? *Foreign* and *foreigner* are words that should be consigned to the list of archaic and misguided epithets we don't use anymore in polite society. Spanish, for example, is hardly "foreign" in the United States. It and the languages from East Asia are growing steadily as common languages spoken in a society where English is the predominant language.

How Are Other Languages Different from English?

The purpose of this section is to show you some basic differences in structure between English and several other languages: Spanish, Vietnamese, Cantonese (the Chinese spoken in the area of Hong Kong), and just a dash of Japanese and Korean. Some of the information may be too specific for your needs, and some of it may not be specific enough, depending on your students. *This information is not meant as a crash course in five languages.* It is intended to provide you with basic information and also to show you some of the ways in which your ESL student is struggling to make sense of English.

Spanish

Perhaps the most glaring difference between English and Spanish, along with the other Romance languages, is that all the nouns in the Romance languages have gender. A door in Spanish is a feminine noun, *la puerta,* while a desk is masculine, *el escritorio.* So it is understandable that a Spanish-speaking student may take a while to get the hang of using the neutral pronoun *it* for inanimate objects. In addition, English nouns don't necessarily take an article *(a, an, the,* none of which appears in, for example, *Trees are part of nature),* whereas Spanish nouns usually do. So Spanish speakers may want to insert an article before nouns that don't take articles in English, and this may sound odd to us, as in *The mister Gonzales isn't here.* Spanish speakers will include an article before a general noun in Spanish, so they might say in English that *The skiing is fun.*

Here are some other common issues for Spanish speakers learning English:

- Learning which prepositions to use poses problems for learners of many languages. In Spanish, *a* is closest to the English prepositions *at* and *to,* and *en* is used where English speakers would say *in, on,* or *at.* So your Spanish speakers might say *He is not in home.*

- You'll hear your Spanish speakers use *that* or *which* when you expect *who: The woman which just came in the room.* The reason is that in Spanish the word *que* is equivalent to *that, which,* and *who.*

- English places the indirect object between the verb and the direct object: *Jack sent Jill a pail of water.* Spanish places the indirect object between the subject and the verb: *Jack Jill sent a pail of water.*

- Spanish places its negative particle before the verb and routinely uses double negatives, leading to such sentences as *She no like the movie* and *He don't like nothing.*

- In English, when we refer to a person, we use the same words whether that person is present or absent. But Spanish speakers use the article to refer to an absent person. In English, that would sound like this: *I saw the Mrs. Benjamin in the grocery store.*

- You may hear Spanish speakers refer to the word *people* in the singular rather than the plural: *The people is angry,* instead of *People are angry.* The reason is that *la gente* is singular in Spanish.

- In English we express possession in one of two ways: we use the possessive apostrophe or the *of* phrase, depending on the kind of thing and the kind of possession we are talking about, as in *the man's beard; the bravery of the people.* The Romance languages use only the *of* phrase: *el libro del nino (the book of the boy).* Considering how much trouble native speakers have with the possessive apostrophe, you can imagine how much trouble a Spanish or French speaker would have with it.

Vietnamese

- The Vietnamese do not place an article before the word for a profession and might say in English, *She is student.*

- Vietnamese does not have the *be* verb. You can expect your Vietnamese students to need help inserting the correct form of *be* in statements and questions.

- A writer of a sentence in Vietnamese will usually place a transitional word between the introductory clause and the main clause. In English, this sounds awkward: *Because she likes to sing, therefore she joined the choir.*

- Vietnamese, like English, uses the subject-verb-object order. Vietnamese, however, omits *it* when referring to weather, distance, and time: *Is raining.* There are no neuter pronouns in Vietnamese.

- In English we express comparison by adding *-er* to the adjective *(bigger)*. In Vietnamese the concept of more is expressed by adding the word for more after the adjective: *The truck big more than the bus.*

- The vowel sounds in the words *hit, bad, shower,* and *hire* are not heard in the Vietnamese language, so a Vietnamese speaker may confuse words with those sounds.

- Expect your Vietnamese students to have some trouble with tense. Vietnamese does not use the same system of expressing events in time. You might hear and read: *We take a trip to Sacramento last summer.* This speaker is using context clues in the sentence to convey the tense, rather than changing the verb as we do in English.

Cantonese

- Cantonese speakers are not accustomed to using helping verbs for questions or negatives. They may be particularly baffled by the English use of *do* in questions and negatives. You may hear this: *How much money this cost?* English speakers don't usually stress that helping verb—*How much <u>does</u> this cost?*—so it is hard for a native Cantonese speaker to hear it. You might need to emphasize the use of the helping verb *do* in questions and negatives.

- Cantonese speakers are likely to be confused by the use of prepositions in English because Cantonese does not use many prepositions. Prepositional use in English is so idiomatic that it may even seem to be random. Why, for example, do we ride *in* a car but *on* a train? Why do we park *in* the parking lot? Why do we hang a picture *on* a wall rather than *against* a wall? Your Cantonese speakers may need to hear you emphasize prepositions in your speech to help them hear the conventions.

- You'll hear your Cantonese speakers placing all of their modifiers up front in the sentence, before the verb: *For her mother on her birthday on Saturday, we gave her a surprise party.*

- Cantonese speakers tend to leave off plurals in English. In Cantonese, Japanese, and Korean, there are no plural forms of nouns: *Many good book.* The difficulty in pronouncing the final *s* is an additional difficulty.

- Cantonese speakers may have trouble with pronouns. They are used to a language with fewer pronouns, many of which are dropped. Because they don't distinguish between subjective and objective forms of pronouns, they may say, *I will give it to they.*

- Parallels of *a*, *an*, and *the* are not used in Cantonese. That is why Cantonese students may erroneously omit the article, as in *I have dog.* They may also insert the article erroneously, as in *I have the pets.*

Korean

- In Korean, pronouns don't have gender, so you might hear Korean-speaking students referring to males and females using the gender-neutral pronoun *it.*
- Korean has no indefinite article but uses *one* for *a*, depending on the context: *He dropped one cup of coffee.*
- Korean, as well as Japanese, places the verb after the subject and object instead of between them as English does. The different order might lead a student to say, *The man the car drove.*

Japanese

- In Japanese, pronouns don't have to match their nouns in terms of singular or plural, so you might have to show the student how to use *we, us, they,* and *them.*
- Japanese, like Cantonese, has no articles and no inflections for person and number: *Teacher give two assignment.*

Summary

To summarize some of the ways that languages can differ from English:

1. The nouns might take gender.
2. Other languages may use articles differently, or no articles at all.
3. Plurals may be formed by adding words or syllables to the sentence, or by giving context clues in the sentence to indicate that there is more than one.
4. The word order may not follow the familiar subject-verb-object pattern.
5. The pronoun may not have to agree in gender or number with its antecedent.
6. Other languages may have fewer prepositions, making it confusing for the novice to know which preposition to use in English. Also, the preposition may not precede its object.
7. There are differences in inflection and pacing.
8. There are differences in written conventions, such as punctuation and capitalization.
9. Nonverbal communications, such as gesture, eye contact, silences, and what people do to indicate that they understand, differ from culture to culture.

What General Strategies Are Helpful with ESL Students?

We teach grammar to help all our students understand language patterns regardless of which language they speak or are trying to speak. Earlier, we described the contrastive approach to helping students with so-called dialect errors, which involves understanding and helping students understand the contrasts in the language patterns of home language and Standard English. Similarly, the teacher confronted by "ESL errors" can try to think about a student's language patterns instead of the individual mistakes. A speaker learning English is almost always testing out a "ground rule" of English. With a little conversation and perhaps some research, you can often discover the intention and the pattern in the student's mind.

Second language students may, for example, say or write *It was happened yesterday* and *He was died.* These sentences—so unlike any that a native speaker would write—are not the result of a sloppy use of the past tense, as they may appear. With some research and discussion with the student, the teacher will realize that the student is adding the *was* out of a mistaken notion that the sentences are in the passive voice; the event seems to be happening to the sentence subject. (Such students would not write *He was kicked the ball,* because the sentence subject is more clearly an active agent.) Once the teacher realizes that the student thinks such sentences require the passive voice, discussing the mistake with the student becomes manageable.

Similarly, ESL students need time to learn the collocations of English, the way that certain words must be accompanied by other words. The collocations of English verbs are especially complex. Some verbs require a direct object and an indirect object (*Give Chris the ball*), some just a direct object (*hit the ball*), and others no object at all (*Chris ran; John walked*). Errors with verb collocations are, in a sense, vocabulary errors, but they lead to grammatical problems. A student might write *Please send tomorrow* and not see it as a sentence fragment because it contains the understood subject of the imperative *(you)* and a tensed verb *(send).* To the student, the sentence is complete, perhaps because in his or her native language the word for *send* does not require a direct object with it. The teacher can explain that in English (except in telegraphic or shorthand prose), it does.

Students whose native language is not English don't automatically realize how much English depends on word order for meaning. Although you take for granted that *The dog bit the man* conveys a different meaning from *The man bit the dog,* an English language learner might not think the difference is so obvious. English is a subject-verb-object language (SVO, for short). Japanese and Korean are subject-object-verb, or SOV, languages. Arabic is a verb-subject-object, or VSO, language. Knowing this difference may help you decipher your students' intended meanings as they learn English.

In English we expect the subject to be stated (except in the case of commands, where the subject "you" is understood, as in *Stop that*). Many other languages do not require the subject to be stated outright; it is expressed by the verb ending. If your English language learners often leave out the subject, you may want to require them to stick to simple SVO sentences, with the subject always stated explicitly.

One more thing about verbs: the most common verbs in English are the irregular ones, those that *don't* follow the usual pattern of adding *-ed* to form the past tense *(walk, walked)*. Be patient with learners who must master *to be, is, am, was, were, are; do, does, did; go, goes, went; buy, bought*; and so on.

Talking about transportation is often a puzzlement for English language learners because of the prepositions *in* and *on*. When the vehicle can carry only one person, or when it carries more than a handful of people, we use *on*: *on* a bicycle, *on* an ocean liner, *on* a train. When a small number of people can ride in a conveyance, we use *in*: *in* a rowboat, *in* a car.

In English the conjunctions *and* and *but* are so common that native speakers take them for granted, but you may need to explain the difference between them for English language learners.

English is rich in metaphors, idioms, and figurative language. You can imagine how these nonliteral expressions would bewilder the novice. An idiom such as *used to (Our library used to be open on Sundays)* is famous for mystifying newcomers to English.

Remember that conventions for capitalization differ from language to language. German capitalizes all nouns. Nationalities are not capitalized in Spanish, Romanian, Russian, or Portuguese. The second word of a geographical place name *(Hudson River)* is not capitalized in Serbo-Croatian and Vietnamese. Not all languages capitalize days of the week or months of the year. And Cantonese, Hindi, and Arabic are among the languages that don't use any capital letters at all.

Not all punctuation looks like English punctuation. Some languages use inverted questions marks, circles, vertical lines, a series of dots, and other markings. Commas don't always appear the way they do in English. In some languages, the comma is inverted, raised, or reversed.

English uses what we call the Roman script. Not all languages use the same script; Arabic, Chinese, Greek, Hindi, Japanese, Korean, Russian, and Tamil are among many hundreds of languages that use different scripts and graphic symbols.

Not all languages have the same rules that English does regarding the joining of independent clauses. Whereas English does not permit two independent clauses to be joined by a comma *(The economy slowly spiraled downward, many people were out of work),* such joinings are permissible in Persian, Arabic, Russian, and Turkish.

English spelling drives native speakers crazy. Imagine what it must be like for speakers of languages such as Spanish and Vietnamese, which have much more consistency. Your ESL students will run into difficulties that you don't expect because their pronunciation conventions differ from those of English speakers. In some languages, for example, the final consonant of a word is not pronounced. If a speaker of such a language carries that practice into English, she or he will be likely to drop the final consonant in spelling as well as in speech in English words. Some languages—Spanish, German, Hindi, for example—are much more phonetic than English, meaning that once you know some basic pronunciation rules, you can usually pronounce a word correctly. In English, think of the challenge the ESL student faces in learning how to pronounce *ough* in *rough, bough, thorough, cough,* and *through.*

In English we have lots of affixes. Other languages, such as many Asian languages, seldom add affixes to words. The notion of a word root such as *tele* (far off) in *telephone,* which has meaning although it does not function as a complete word, is unfamiliar.

Your non-native speakers will have problems enough with the irregularities of English spelling. You can help them learn spelling by working with them on their pronunciation. Doing this doesn't always necessitate correcting them. Simply clarifying or slightly exaggerating your own pronunciation of tricky words will be helpful.

Chinese and Vietnamese do not pluralize words. These languages convey the plural through the context of the sentence. Romance languages do have plurals, but the plurals are formed according to rules which are much more consistent than the rules in English. Be aware that ESL students may find English plurals difficult.

Homonyms (words that sound alike but that have different and often unrelated meanings, such as *the <u>bear</u> in the woods* and *to <u>bear</u> a burden*) don't exist in all languages.

The second-language student may have difficulty adjusting to the rhetorical patterns of composition that English teachers take for granted.

This difficulty occurs not only when the student has learned to read or write in another language but also as the result of absorbing ways of talking and thinking that are organized differently in other cultures. Compared to American rhetorical patterns, for instance, Asian cultures tend to use fewer explicit thesis statements throughout a piece of writing, while Spanish writing allows for more changes in the direction of the discussion. Such patterns that vary from traditional English ones are, in their respective countries, regarded as sensible and prestigious, and from these other points of view the English expository pattern of main idea followed by supporting details appears rigid and limiting. Try to learn about such contrastive rhetoric so that you can help students through this aspect of their cultural reorientation.

Finally, we need to keep in mind that the nonverbal cues of communication differ from culture to culture. Most Americans expect the person to whom they are speaking to make eye contact; not to do so is considered a sign of disrespect. In some cultures, making eye contact is a sign of confrontation; casting one's eyes downward when an authority is speaking signifies proper deference.

What Are Some Specific Ways You Can Help?

- To help ESL students learn how to use nouns and adjectives, have them write descriptions.

- To help ESL students learn how to use pronouns, have them write narratives about themselves and their friends.

- On the student's perspective: Ask the student to write about writing. Depending on the student's age and mastery of English, the student can write about those sentence structures that she or he finds difficult. The student can write in English or in the native language or in both. Ask the student to explain whether the mistakes are caused by the influence of the native language or by a misunderstanding of an English pattern. Also, students can keep a running list of English words they look up in the dictionary.

- On the editing of writing: Don't succumb to the attitude that just because an English language learner is making more or different errors compared to native speakers, the student needs you as the ultimate proofreader and he or she will not benefit from working on writing with classmates. Peer editing partnerships and groups can work well for students from other cultures, many of which encourage young people to help one another with schoolwork. Similarly, just because a student makes ESL errors, don't focus any less on the content and meaning in the writing of ESL students than on the same aspects of the writing of native speakers. And, for the same reason, don't neglect extended writing assignments for ESL writers; it's not true that they have to write the perfect sentence before the paragraph and the perfect paragraph before the story or essay.

- Keep your explanations brief and simple. Illustrate with clear, unambiguous examples. Do not get yourself (and students) tied up in knots over exceptions to rules. Use visuals, but explain them verbally.

- If a student asks you about a point of English grammar and you aren't sure what the answer is or how to explain it simply and clearly, don't rush. Tell the student you will bring back an answer at the next class period.

- Be aware of the effects of your speech. Be aware of those occasions with beginning speakers when they will understand you better if you speak a little slowly and emphasize your meaning with gestures or facial expressions (although you don't want to appear to be talking down to them). Similarly, they may understand you more easily when you speak in short sentences and when you use the active instead of the passive voice.

- Include definitions of unfamiliar terms within your sentences.

- To help all students become more sophisticated about language variations, avoid using terms such as *substandard, wrong, broken English, illiterate,* and other pejorative terms that discount the value of linguistic variation. Instead, use terms such as *colloquial, informal, regional, vernacular,* and *inappropriate for this context.* Stress the importance of using the language tone geared toward a particular audience and situation.

- To help all students learn more about languages, point out cognates and Latin roots. This will also help native English speakers learn and remember new words.

- Talk about words borrowed from other languages. Help ESL students find words in English borrowed from their languages: *bazaar, café, caribou, macho, mantra, safari, smorgasbord, sabotage, shogun, wok,* etc.

- On tapping ESL students as a classroom grammar resource: Are you discussing verb number with your class? Noun endings? Punctuation? Invite a student with a different language background to speak about his or her own language. Very often, such students can respond with clear and interesting comments because they may know grammatical terminology (as a result of their ESL studies) better than most native speakers do.

- Be aware that the English language is full of idioms that baffle the novice.

- Model a positive, open-minded attitude about language variation. Doing so is one of the most powerful ways that you can teach for social justice.

Conclusion

One of the goals of education should be to make every high school graduate bidialectical. What this means is that everyone should have two language varieties, the informal, more private speech they use with family and friends, and the public, formal language of the business world and formal occasions. For ESL students, their private speech at home is an entirely different language from public English, and so their challenge in mastering two sets of language skills is more complex than it is for native English speakers.

For us as teachers, this goal makes our task more complex as well. On the one hand, it is incumbent upon us as educators to help our students communicate in a way that will not put them at risk of being thought ignorant or unsophisticated when they travel from place to place or from level to level in the professional world. On the other hand, nothing is more personal to our students, and to us, than our language and the language of our family, loved ones, ethnic group, and community. So this is a sensitive area. It is imperative that we feel and show a genuine respect for other languages and language dialects and for the difficult process of learning English as a new language. We suppress language variety at our peril, as our suppression feeds a sense of alienation from education and public discourse, the last thing any educator wants.

VIGNETTE: TEACHING ENGLISH LANGUAGE LEARNERS IN ELEMENTARY GRADES

In helping young children whose native language is not English, it is difficult to figure out—among the other challenges—whether to include direct instruction in grammar and if so, how. Here, a third-grade teacher decides that grammar will be only a small piece of her larger strategy, and her approach conflicts with that of another teacher. Have you thought through your own beliefs about the place of grammar instruction in such situations?

Kathleen J., a young third-grade teacher in a suburban school, is a perfectionist by nature. When a problem comes along, she uses every resource available to solve it. When state budget cuts knocked the wind out of her district, instruction time for English language learners (ELL) was reduced to just two forty-minute sessions per week for children whose native language was not English. So Katherine decided she had no choice but to become a second ELL teacher for Nhan, the Chinese-speaking girl new to the district.

Kathleen consulted with the ELL specialist and gave herself a crash course in teaching English as a second language, knowing that she would have many children like Nhan in her teaching career. She even tried to learn a few words in Chinese, but they flew right out of her head almost as soon as she pronounced them. Kathleen settled on three practical teaching strategies to maximize Nhan's learning of English: patience, socialization, and reading aloud.

Fluency takes time. Nhan was quiet. Kathleen was patient. Children learning English are likely to absorb language for a long time without saying much. But, like a toddler who understands much more of what is said than she can express herself, Nhan was constructing meaning from the social relationships that Kathleen encouraged. Kathleen explained this to the other children, some of whom were beginning to interpret Nhan's reticence as unfriendliness. "She likes you," Kathleen explained. "She just needs to be ready to talk."

Kathleen's research and observation convinced her that Nhan would learn English just fine, given the time and the social context. Then she ran into a new problem. The ELL specialist left the district to find a full-time position elsewhere. The new ELL teacher believed in workbooks, fill-ins, drills, and the traditional rules of English grammar. She insisted that her program was a tried-and-true means of teaching "correct" grammar. Kathleen tried to help Nhan with her workbook exercises. Nhan was correctly filling in the blanks, but the work didn't seem to transfer to her conversational speech, which is what Nhan really needed help with. Kathleen was patient, but she had more faith that the modeling Nhan was getting from her peers in social conversation would eventually find its way into Nhan's speech.

Meanwhile, Kathleen read aloud to Nhan and had peers read aloud to her as well. The reading aloud had several benefits. Nhan heard and emulated the rhythms of speech, something the workbooks didn't give her. Instruction about basic grammar (how the English language works) sometimes became part of the discussion of the story as Kathleen pointed to the -*s* endings on certain nouns and verbs.

▶

Nhan developed confidence in using English as she memorized parts of the stories and recited them, first along with the reader's voice and then on her own.

Kathleen began to elicit English from Nhan by asking her questions about the pictures in her books. Nhan responded with single nouns at first, then with phrases and sentences about the stories she knew. She was using known information in the stories to learn new information as she began to talk about the stories on her own. To Kathleen, the process felt much like the ritual of reading aloud to toddlers, asking them questions, and using their familiarity with the language and objects of the story to introduce new vocabulary and grammatical structures in the course of natural conversation.

Nhan's classmates were delighted when she began to participate in reading groups as a "reader." (She recited from memory.) Kathleen advised them to accept Nhan's mispronunciations, modeling for them how to "show" standard pronunciation through their own speech rather than "tell" Nhan how to pronounce a word.

As the year progressed, Kathleen was satisfied with what Nhan was able to understand, say, and read. In her teaching journal, she noted the following positive strategies:

1. Use language experiences with rhythm and rhyme; read aloud a lot.
2. Use dramatics: skits, puppets, dolls, and action figures.
3. Don't be discouraged by silences and backsliding.
4. Correct grammatical errors by modeling, not direct teaching.
5. Teach the child the polite conventions that English speakers use to ask for help: "Could you repeat that, please?"; "Please explain what you mean"; "Excuse me, what do you mean by that?"
6. Focus on the three Rs: repetition, rewording, reinforcement.

Kathleen's experience with Nhan and subsequent experience with other English language learners taught her an amazing amount about the English language and the human brain: the many grammatical ways there are to manipulate a sentence; the importance of inflection; how much of conversational English is idiomatic; the confusing nature of phrasal verbs; how hard it is to explain certain prepositions. Whereas the ELL specialist addressed the English language part by part and topic by topic, Kathleen used immersion theory.

Learning a language, acclimating to a new culture, making new friends, and learning a curriculum is a lot to do all at once for an eight-year-old child. But with friendly support from her peers and teacher, Nhan learned each new task, which helped her learn others.

—Amy Benjamin

VIGNETTE: HELPING A NINTH-GRADE STUDENT USE *THE*

Working from a student's paper, a ninth-grade teacher tries to strike a balance between direct instruction and student discovery to help a boy from Costa Rica master a challenging piece of English usage. English, like all languages, includes usage patterns that native speakers never have to think about but that non-native speakers must sometimes study explicitly. Which everyday usage patterns do the non-native speakers in your class have difficulty with in writing or speaking? Of these, are there any whose rules you think you yourself should find out more about so you can explain to the student exactly what to do?

Ms. Sabo is meeting with her ninth grader Raphael, a student from Costa Rica who has been attending U.S. schools for the last five years. Raphael, like many students who grew up with languages other than English, is still struggling with some aspects of the English article system. Ms. Sabo goes over the opening paragraph of his paper with him.

> In Costa Rica I had a friend in our town. We talked about the nature. The farms were all around our town. We talked about how the coffee grows, and we saw that the nature has a lot of secrets. We became the best friends. He told me many proverbs and I remember them. They help me to understand more about the life.

Raphael is putting the definite article *the* in front of nouns that normally don't take it. The general principle in English is that *the* is omitted before nouns that are uncountable (*coffee* and many other food names, for example), plural countable nouns when their meaning is

▶

generalized *(Elephants are large,* in contrast to *The elephants are large),* and many but not all singular proper nouns *(Italy,* but *the Nile).* Ms. Sabo has looked up the principles of article use so that she can help students like Raphael. Moreover, she thinks Raphael himself has probably heard these rules in the past in his ESL courses. But she knows that the patterns of English usage take time to absorb.

"Raphael, you're putting *the* in some places where you don't need it. In English we don't use *the* before certain kinds of words that are very general. Let's look at *nature.* You've written *We talked about the nature* and *the nature has a lot of secrets.* Let me ask you, if you are walking in the woods, where is nature?"

"It's in the trees. It's kind of . . . everywhere," Raphael replies.

"Right. It's everywhere. So *nature* is a very general noun. We talk about nature but we are not talking about a specific place or specific trees. It is not possible, really, to go and point to a nature here and a nature there. You can't count how many natures there are. We don't say 'two natures' or 'three natures' in English. There is just 'nature.'"

Raphael listens but doesn't say anything. Ms. Sabo thinks about another example.

"Let's take the word *poetry.* I know you have liked the poetry we've read in class. You enjoyed the poems and you said once that poems were like puzzles. So you might say to me, 'I like . . . ' what? How would you say that sentence using the word *poetry*?"

"'I like poetry.' Can I say 'I like poetry in our book'"?

"You would say 'I like *the* poetry in our book' because that's a few specific poems. But your first answer was right. You would say 'I like poetry' if you want to say that you think you like poetry in general, as a whole."

"Okay."

"In your paper, you wrote *They help me to understand more about the life.* Can you tell me if you think you should take out the *the* before *life,* or not?"

Raphael replies, "I think I should keep it in because I am talking about my life."

"Are you talking about just your life by yourself or about what life is like for other people as well as you?"

"Oh, okay, I see, it's life in a big way." Raphael nods, and Ms. Sabo nods with him.

▷

"Yes, that's it. *They help me to understand more about life.* Now let's look at one more example for today. You wrote *We became the best friends.* This example is more complicated. Sometimes you *can* say 'the best friends.' For instance, it's good English to say or write, 'They were the best friends that I ever had.' But when you say 'We became the best friends,' you're being more general again. It's the same when you say 'We became friends.' Or 'We became buddies' or 'We became teammates.'

"What about 'We became family'?" Raphael asks.

Ms. Sabo is stumped for a moment. She's not sure if he is thinking of the informal use of that phrase, as in the song "We Are Family," or if he is making an error in the sentence *We became a family.* She decides to keep the focus on the most standard usage and not get sidetracked by exceptions.

"Usually, when a specific event has happened, like a man and woman having a baby, they say 'We have become a family.'"

"Okay."

"Raphael, for tomorrow, I would like you to go through your paper and look at the other nouns with *the* in front of them. Put a circle around those nouns and think about whether they are general or not. It's a complicated part of English, so don't get discouraged. Most of your other English grammar is very good. I'll see you tomorrow."

Ms. Sabo isn't sure how much of the explanation Raphael has absorbed or how he is hearing certain sentences. But she's encouraged by some of his answers. She will know more tomorrow. She'll bring up the terms *countable* and *uncountable* if all goes well—the words *general* and *specific* work well enough for simple explanations, but they can be difficult to explain with precision. And once Raphael has had some time to think about using *the*, she will encourage him to talk more about how he is understanding the nouns and to come up with examples of different types of nouns on his own.

—Brock Haussamen, with Christine Herron

ESL Resources

Burt, Marina K., and Carol Kiparsky. *The Gooficon: A Repair Manual for English.* Rowley, MA: Newbury House, 1972. A listing of grammar mistakes and a guide to understanding and addressing them.

Celce-Murcia, Marianne, and Dianne Larsen-Freeman, with Howard Williams. *The Grammar Book: An ESL/EFL Teacher's Course.* 2nd ed. Boston:

Heinle & Heinle, 1999. This comprehensive guide to grammar for the ESL teacher is more than the language arts teacher needs, but it includes two valuable resources. The first is an index of English words and phrases discussed in the text; an English teacher can use this index to find information about the language issues involved in a particular construction that a second-language student may be using. Second, at the end of each chapter are teaching suggestions on the chapter's grammar topic.

Friedlander, Alexander. "Composing in English: Effects of a First Language on Writing in English as a Second Language." *Second Language Writing: Research Insights for the Classroom.* Ed. Barbara Kroll. Cambridge, UK: Cambridge University Press, 1990. A study showing that, depending on the assignment, ESL students sometimes generate better English compositions when they plan their papers using their first language than when they try to do so in English.

Leki, Ilona. *Understanding ESL Writers: A Guide for Teachers.* Portsmouth, NH: Boynton/Cook, 1992. Highly recommended.

Martin, James E. *Towards a Theory of Text for Contrastive Rhetoric: An Introduction to Issues of Text for Students and Practitioners of Contrastive Rhetoric.* New York: Peter Lang, 1992. This book describes the field of contrastive rhetoric, the study of the differences in how people in different cultures use text and organize their discourse.

Raimes, Ann. "Anguish as a Second Language? Remedies for Composition Teachers." *Composing in a Second Language.* Ed. Sandra McKay. Rowley, MA: Newbury House, 1984. Process-approach strategies for writing teachers helping second language learners.

Richard-Amato, Patricia A., and Marguerite Ann Snow, eds. *The Multicultural Classroom: Readings for Content-Area Teachers.* White Plains, NY: Longman, 1992. Many essays in this collection will be just as useful to the language arts teacher as to the content-area teacher. See especially "Coaching the Developing Second Language Writer" by Faye Peitzman and "Providing Culturally Sensitive Feedback" by Robin Scarcella.

Rigg, Pat, and Virginia G. Allen, eds. *When They Don't All Speak English: Integrating the ESL Student into the Regular Classroom.* Urbana, IL: National Council of Teachers of English, 1989. A collection of ten essays.

Finally, the Web site www.stanford.edu/~kenro/LAU/ICLangLit/NaturalApproach.htm#Monitor is a useful introduction to the work of Stephen Krashen, an influential and controversial figure in ESL who advocates a "natural approach" to teaching grammar. The Web site offers a good summary of the issue, a strong critique, and a bibliography. The section on the Monitor hypothesis describes the potential usefulness for ESL students of grammar rules as monitors for editing their work under certain conditions.

II On Grammar

The first part of this book focused on classroom approaches to grammar. The chapters in this part focus more on information you may want about grammar itself and about stylistic issues related to grammar. These chapters provide answers to questions such as "Is it considered acceptable to use *you* in writing essays?" (Chapter 6, "Grammar Superstitions"); "How does sentence diagramming work?" (Chapter 7, "Diagramming Sentences"); "What exactly is a noun phrase?" (Chapter 8, "An Overview of Linguistic Grammar"). In addition, you can consult the grammar glossary near the end of the book for definitions and examples of grammar terms.

   Of the three chapters in Part II, the overview of linguistic grammar (Chapter 8) contains by far the most information. It amounts to a minicourse in current structural grammar, written by Martha Kolln, a coauthor of the widely used textbook *Understanding English Grammar* and the author of the textbook *Rhetorical Grammar: Grammatical Choices, Rhetorical Effects*. The chapter describes word classes (the two basic types of words), sentence constituents (the noun phrases and verb phrases that make up all sentences), sentence patterns (the seven patterns of English sentences), and the verb system of African American English (verb forms that may seem haphazard but in reality make up a regular and consistent system of their own). This is the chapter that will provide you—when you want it and are ready for some concentrated reading—with a solid foundation of formal knowledge about grammar.

6 Grammar Superstitions: The Never-Never Rules

For many of us, "grammar" is all about the things you should never do: Never end a sentence with a preposition. Never split an infinitive. Never use a contraction. Never begin a sentence with *and*, *but*, or *because*. Never refer to yourself as "I" or address your reader as "you." But any look at professional writing, the kind of writing that lives and breathes, will reveal the folly of the Never-Never Rules. They are merely hobgoblins and superstitions.

The Never-Never Rules prevail in many English classrooms probably because English teachers learned them and feel an obligation to pass them on. (Try twisting that sentence into a pretzel to avoid violating the final preposition "rule.") But follow them to the letter and all you are likely to end with is writing that is stilted, voiceless, and uninviting. The Never-Never Rules might have made sense once, somewhere, sometime, for somebody (they were usually stylistic suggestions that eighteenth-century writers and grammarians became increasingly dogmatic about). But over time, language changes. Over space, language varies. The wise writing teacher watches language as it is actually used and is not haunted by superstitions.

Let's look at some of the Never-Never Rules one by one:

1. The Dreaded Sentence-Ending Preposition

The superstition that a sentence should not end with a preposition grew out of a somewhat reasonable piece of eighteenth-century advice that an effectively written sentence should not end with a weak or unimportant word. But in the nineteenth century, the advice about final prepositions hardened into a stern grammar rule, and despite the best efforts of some major writers and commentators to get rid of it, it unfortunately endures. Even Winston Churchill tried to put this superstition to rest. When he was criticized for a sentence of his that ended with a preposition, he retorted, "That is the type of arrant pedantry up with which I shall not put!"

Even in the eighteenth century, grammarians understood that although its Latin name suggested that a *pre-position* was positioned *before* its object, English prepositions were often more closely connected to the verbs they came *after*. Take the sentence *We were talking to Ricardo.*

When you form the question *Is Ricardo the person you were talking to?*, the affinity between the verb and the preposition—*talking to*—is clear. And the question *Is Ricardo the person to whom you were talking?* simply seems to deny one of the great strengths of the English language, its flexible word order.

Moreover, hundreds of common English verbs include what is known as a particle as an integral part of the verb itself. Such phrases are *phrasal verbs.* (The particles are words that also serve as prepositions and adverbs, so it is no wonder that many people are unsure how to view phrasal verbs.) Think of all the phrasal verbs we use that are formed from just the one verb *take: take after, take apart, take back, take down, take for, take in, take off, take on, take out, take over, take to,* and *take up* (these are all listed in the *American Heritage Dictionary* as *take*'s phrasal verbs). Some phrasal verbs are separable: we can say, "Take out the garbage" or "Take the garbage out." Others—sentences that end in what look like prepositions and that are impossible to change unless you alter the words—include *The dinosaurs died off; Cheap loans are not easy to come by;* and *I hope a riot doesn't break out.*

Phrasal verbs are essential components of smooth, informal English prose. You can help your students by asking them to keep a record of phrasal verbs so that they feel encouraged to use them and so that they understand them clearly as a type of verb. You'll also be helping to put one bothersome grammar superstition to rest.

2. The Abhorred Split Infinitive

To split an infinitive is to insert an adverb between *to* and the verb, as in *to boldly go.* To acquire a sane and relaxed attitude about this so-called rule is *to boldly go* where few teachers have dared to go before.

So what's wrong with splitting an infinitive? Nothing, really. It is time (and has been time for some two hundred years now) *to firmly lay* to rest any injunctions now enforced against the so-called splitting of infinitives. And since we are permitted to split infinitives, we really have no use for the term itself.

Why has such a superstition survived for so long? Probably because, like the final preposition, the split infinitive is easy to spot. For those in the past who wanted to fuss about grammar but weren't too sure that they really understood it, detecting both errors was just a matter of looking at word order: the *to* followed by the adverb, the little preposition at the end of the sentence. You don't have to know much about grammar to find those constructions and call them errors. But we should know better.

3. The Contraction of Ill-Repute

Contractions soften the writer's voice. To write without contractions is to deliver a standoffish, unrhythmical, overly formalized style that won't ease the reader's journey to understanding. Although it's true that students need to learn the academic voice that separates serious writing from instant messaging, it's also true that the common contractions appear in plenty of serious books and essays. The "do not use contractions" method of achieving high-sounding prose is shallow and only leads to other superficial fix-ups. It's no substitute for helping a student improve the tone of his or her writing with richer diction and more varied sentence structure.

4. Three Little Words: And, But, So

As fledgling writers learn how to connect one sentence to another, they make a few errors regarding clause boundaries. If ideas are flowing nicely from sentence to sentence, they may even emulate professional writers and begin a few sentences with the coordinating conjunctions *and, but,* or *so.* The word *but* especially is such an easy and succinct way to open a sentence with a new direction that one finds plentiful examples in most professional writing. *But* if we slash our students' papers in red for writing in the style they read, we send them one of two absurd messages: either all of these professionals are wrong and never learned their sentence-starting rules, or there must be some kind of graduate club of writers that students are denied access to.

Better we should just tell them the truth: Beginning sentences with coordinating conjunctions lends an air of informality that may or may not be welcome, depending on the audience, occasion, and purpose. It is far more educationally sound to have students deduce, from real text, circumstances in which writers never begin any sentences with conjunctions and other circumstances in which they do so freely. They can also describe the rhetorical or stylistic effects of opening sentences this way.

The same logic applies for the much-maligned yet ubiquitous one-sentence paragraph.

5. The Impudent I

We want students to develop voice, right? Then why are we taking away their personal pronoun? If you look carefully at your students' writing, you are likely to find that some of their worst moments result from avoiding a touch of first person: ineffective use of the passive, the stuffy use of "one" or "an individual," and other distancing mechanisms—leading to such clunkers as *There was a party last weekend attended by many of the juniors.*

The first-person pronoun can be used unobtrusively, tastefully, in the service of conciseness. It is a natural term to use when the writer is the center of an action or a thought. From Martin Luther King Jr.'s "I Have a Dream" speech: "But there is something that I must say to my people who stand on the warm threshold which leads into the palace of justice."

6. *The Unconscionable* You

Just as we want students to write *from* a real self, we also want them to write *to* a real audience. To *you*. *You* language is direct, personalized, focused, and purposeful. It invites you in, speaks to your needs, makes you feel that a real person is talking to you. You might have noticed that it plays an important part in the style and tone of the book you are reading. Encourage your students to care about their subjects and their readers by using *you* accurately and often to address the reader.

Here's the point: Writing is good or bad only to the extent that it suits its intended audience for a particular occasion and purpose. As teachers, we need to teach students to suit their style of writing to the many rhetorical modes through which writers and readers come together: personal narrative, academic essay, description, persuasive essay, reportage, lab reports, technical and scientific writing, etc. Each mode tends to have its own voice, a voice determined by grammatical choices that alter the relationship between writer and reader.

For more guidance on these and other grammar superstitions, as well as sound explanations of acceptable practice in standard American usage, spelling, and punctuation, see Bryan Garner's *The Oxford Dictionary of American Usage and Style.*

7 Diagramming Sentences

In the late nineteenth century, Alonzo Reed and Brainerd Kellogg developed a method for diagramming sentences in the belief that students would understand sentence structure better if they could picture it. Many students do indeed find the diagrams helpful in seeing the relationships among sentence elements. (Linguists today, though, prefer another type of diagram that looks like a pyramid.) Here are some suggestions for using the Reed-Kellogg diagrams in your classes:

- Use diagrams as you go along teaching grammar so that they become your regular method for illustrating the basic parts of a sentence. If you try to teach diagramming as an added grammar lesson after students have already worked at becoming familiar with the concepts, many of them may find it tedious.

- Sentence diagramming will test your sense of your students' different learning styles. For students who are visual organizers, the diagrams can be very satisfying, an exercise in problem analysis that they enjoy enormously. For others, the spatial arrangement just doesn't help. You will need to find out which students react in which ways and adjust your assignments and exercises accordingly.

- Remember that sentence diagramming (like grammar study in general) is a means to an end, not an end in itself. Teach what will help students make sense of how actual sentences are organized. Sometimes the diagram of just the sentence core— the head of the subject phrase and the head of the main verb phrase—will help students see more clearly.

- Sentence diagrams can make good collaborative projects. Students can argue about them, make posters of the patterns, or try their hand (if they like diagrams) at diagramming famous sentences from the Declaration of Independence, the Gettysburg Address, and so forth.

- The horizontal line of the diagram has been compared to a spine, with the verb and the whole predicate as the backbone and the subject as the head. Not a perfect metaphor, but one your students might like to work with.

1. The main line of the diagram shows the head noun of the subject divided from the predicate by a vertical line running through the horizontal. After the verb, a shorter vertical line divides the verb from the head noun of the direct object.

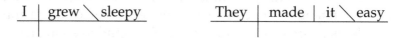

2. A diagonal line, leaning toward the noun it refers to, precedes the subject or object complement.

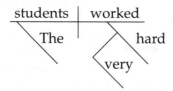

3. Modifiers appear on diagonal lines below the appropriate words on the main line. Qualifiers are placed on diagonal lines attached to the modifiers.

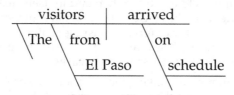

4. A preposition is placed on a diagonal line beneath the word it modifies. The object of the preposition appears on a horizontal line attached to the line of the preposition.

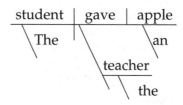

5. An indirect object is set up like a prepositional phrase because its meaning can be expressed by the prepositions *to* or *for*, although the preposition is not written in unless it appears in the sentence. The indirect object is placed below the verb.

6. Conjunctions appear as dashed lines connecting parallel elements.

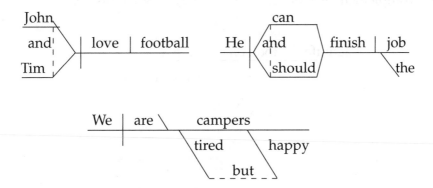

7. Dashed lines also connect clauses to the main sentence elements that they modify. A relative pronoun is placed in its appropriate slot in the relative (adjectival) clause. Subordinating conjunctions are written on the dashed lines.

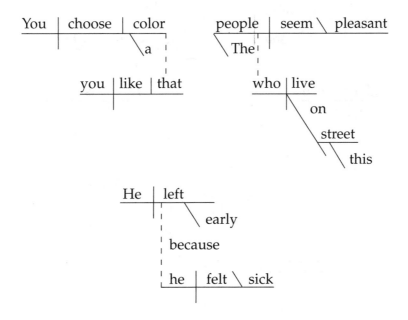

8. An infinitive phrase—with *to* followed by a verb with its modifiers and complements—looks similar to a prepositional phrase.

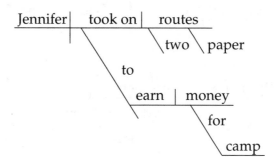

9. Phrases and clauses that occupy the subject or complement slot are written on pedestals above the main clause.

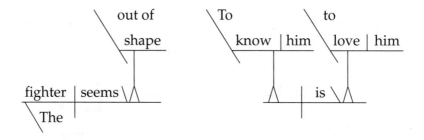

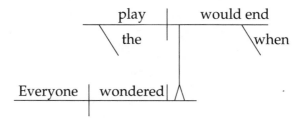

10. The two clauses of a compound sentence are connected with a dashed line from verb to verb, with the conjunction on a solid line between the two.

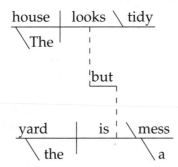

This description of diagramming, from Kolln and Funk's *Understanding English Grammar,* includes slight variations from the original Reed and Kellogg diagrams. Kolln and Funk's text also includes diagrams of many other, and more complex, grammatical structures.

8 An Overview of Linguistic Grammar

The purpose of this chapter is to acquaint you with concepts of linguistic grammar that you may find useful in your teaching. We are using the term *linguistic grammar* to distinguish this description from that of traditional grammar, the Latin-based description that has dominated school grammar for several centuries. We are not suggesting that you substitute this grammar for what is already familiar to you. Rather, we hope that you'll find either additional or alternative ways of describing the structure of sentences, ways that take advantage of our subconscious knowledge of language structure.

Word Classes

When linguists looked at English sentences objectively, rather than through the lens of Latin, with its eight parts of speech, they classified words into two broad categories:

1. *Form classes:* nouns, verbs, adjectives, and adverbs. These "open" classes, which constitute perhaps 99 percent of our language, are open to new members, with nouns and verbs and adjectives and adverbs entering the language as new technology and new ideas require them.

2. *Structure classes:* determiners, auxiliaries, qualifiers, prepositions, conjunctions, and pronouns. In general, these are the "closed" classes; they remain constant. While it's true we no longer hear *whilst* and *betwixt* and *thy,* we have managed with the same fairly small store of structure words that Shakespeare used. Although the form classes have more members, the structure classes are by far the most frequently used; in fact, our twenty most frequently used words are all structure-class words.

Another difference between the two classes is their function in the sentence: the form classes provide the primary lexical meaning, while the structure classes provide the grammatical, or structural, relationships. We can compare the two classes to the bricks and mortar of a building: the form classes are the bricks, the structure classes the mortar that holds them together. Consider, for example, lines from Lewis Carroll's "Jabberwocky":

> T'was brillig and the slithy toves
> Did gyre and gimble in the wabe

All of the nonsense words are form-class words; their form and their position, of course, help give them meaning. But without the structure words, "Jabberwocky" would have no meaning at all:

> brillig slithy toves
> gyre gimble wabe

Notice, too, that when you read these words without the clues of the structure words, the sentences (if you can call them that) lose their rhythm. Most structure words are unstressed: they have the lowest volume and pitch, providing valleys between the peaks of loudness that fall on the stressed syllables of form-class words. As native speakers, or experienced second language speakers, we don't have to pay much attention to the structure classes, but we certainly miss them when they're gone. And they are no doubt the most difficult for non-native speakers to master.

The Form Classes

Nouns, verbs, adjectives, and adverbs get the label "form classes" because they have inflectional forms (such as verbs with tense endings) and derivational forms (those with prefixes and some suffixes) that differentiate them from one another as well as from the other classes. These prefixes and suffixes illustrate the internal "rules" of grammar that native speakers begin learning in their earliest stages of speech, rules they follow automatically. (Young children who say "goed" and "sheeps" are demonstrating their knowledge of the inflectional rules.) Bringing these rules into the classroom will help students develop a conscious understanding of the parts of speech. What follows is a brief description of the inflectional and derivational affixes.

Inflectional Suffixes

Nouns: the plural -*s* and the possessive -*s*. Not every noun has a plural form (e.g., *chaos, tennis, happiness*) and many nouns are rarely, if ever, used with the possessive -*s*; however, any word that can be made plural and/or possessive is, by definition, a noun.

Verbs: -*s, -ed, -en,* and -*ing*. With perhaps two exceptions (*rumor* and *beware* come to mind), all verbs have these four inflections. The -*ed* inflection forms the past tense; the -*s* form is the present-tense form used with a third-person singular subject. As main verbs, the -*ing* and -*en* endings require particular auxiliaries: a form of *have* takes the *-en* form of the verb *(has eaten);* a form of *be* takes the *-ing (am eating).* A "regular" verb is one in which both the *-ed* and *-en* inflections are *-ed (I walked to the store; I have walked to the store).* We also have about 150 verbs with "irregular" *-en* and *-ed* endings, most of which are among our most common verbs, including *be, have, do, say, make, go, take, come, see, get, put,* and *beat.* To figure out the *-ed* (past) ending, simply use the form that would work with *Yesterday: Yesterday we made cookies; Yesterday Joe took me to the movies.* To figure out the *-en* form, simply use a form of *have* as an auxiliary: *We have made cookies already; Joe has taken me to the movies many times.* Other than the irregular verbs, however, all verbs have these five forms: *walk, walks, walked, walked, walking.* In terms of form, the verb is the most systematic word class in English.

 Adjectives: the comparative degree, *-er,* and the superlative, *-est.* In the case of adjectives of more than one syllable, the words *more* and *most* generally substitute for *-er* and *-est.* When Lewis Carroll has Alice saying "curiouser and curiouser," he does so for comic effect. The adjective inflections, however, are not nearly as systematic as those for verbs; that is, many adjectives do not have degrees. We do not, for example, say "more main" or "mainest." Others in this category that do not take inflections include *principal, former, mere, potential, atomic,* and such technical adjectives as *sulfuric.*

 Adverbs: As with adjectives, some adverbs have inflections for the comparative *-er* (or *more*) and the superlative *-est (most)* degrees. Among those that can be inflected are adverbs that are identical to adjectives: *hard, fast, early, late, high, low,* and *deep.* Another group commonly inflected are the adverbs of manner, produced when *-ly* is added to the adjective: *quickly, slowly, correctly, helpfully, beautifully, badly.* There are also a great many common adverbs denoting time, location, direction, and such that have no inflections: *now, then, here, there, everywhere, inside, seldom, never,* etc.

Derivational Affixes

All of the other suffixes (other than the eight inflectional ones just discussed) and all of the prefixes are called "derivational"—that is, they enable us to derive a new part of speech or a new meaning. (The inflectional suffixes do not change the word class.) Even in the absence of semantic meaning, it's safe to assume that the *-y* on *slithy* in "Jabberwocky" turned a noun *(slith)* into an adjective (compare *healthy* and *greasy* and *funny*). Following are some of the most common derivational affixes that help us recognize and use the form classes:

Nouns: -tion and its variations (*-sion, -ion, -ation,* etc.), *-ment, -ness, -ance, -al, -age, -er: abolition, movement, happiness, acceptance, arrival, breakage, teacher*

Verbs: -ify, -en, en-, -ate, -ize: typify, darken, enact, activate, legalize

Adjectives: -ous, -y, -ful, -ate, -ish, -ary, -ive, -able: famous, funny, playful, fortunate, selfish, imaginary, active, lovable

Adverbs: -ly: quickly. It's important to recognize that the *-ly* adverbs are made from adjectives. But not all *-ly* words are adverbs: *friendly* and *lovely* are both adjectives in which the *-ly* has been added to a noun; *bully* and *folly* are nouns.

The Structure Classes

Determiners: Determiners signal, or mark, nouns. The presence of *the* or *a(n)* signals the beginning of a noun phrase. Consider, for example, the noun markers in the sentence you just read:

> <u>The</u> presence of *the* or *a(n)* signals <u>the</u> beginning of <u>a</u> noun phrase.

We generally think of these determiners, the articles *a* and *the,* as the quintessential determiners: determiner is their only role.

Possessive pronouns and possessive nouns also function as determiners: *my* book; *Susie's* bicycle. Other common determiners are the demonstrative pronouns (*this, that, these,* and *those*) and indefinite pronouns (*some, many, each, every, all,* etc.). These groups, along with the cardinal numbers (*one, two, three,* etc.), are the principal structure words in the determiner category. All of them will appear at the start of a noun phrase, in front of any adjectives that modify the noun (*a big, glass table; every pepperoni pizza; two delightful dogs*).

At this point, we should emphasize that the label "determiner" does not denote a clear-cut "part of speech" as "conjunction" and "preposition" do. Rather, it denotes both a word class and a function. (In fact, the early structural grammarians called these classes "function" rather than "structure" classes.) Words such as *my,* of course, are members of the pronoun class; words such as *Susie's* are members of the noun class.

Recognizing this subclass of structure words as noun signalers helps students use their subconscious language ability when they consider sentence structure in a conscious way, not only when they are discussing grammar but also when they write. Our use of the article is a good example. The selection of the definite article (*the*) rather than the indefinite (*a* or *an*) often distinguishes between a known and an unknown referent, a distinction that native speakers generally make without thinking, but one that second language learners must learn consciously. In many instances, we use the indefinite article at the first mention of a noun and the definite article in subsequent mentions:

> There's <u>a</u> big black dog on the porch. I wonder who <u>the</u> dog belongs to.

The determiner can certainly contribute to the cohesion of a text. For example, as the first word in the noun phrase, and thus frequently the first word of the sentence and even of the paragraph, the determiner can bridge ideas in a variety of ways, making subtle but important distinctions and helping readers move from one idea to the next:

> <u>This</u> attempt to solve the problem proved futile.
>
> <u>The</u> attempt to solve the problem . . .
>
> <u>Their</u> attempt . . .
>
> <u>One</u> such attempt . . .
>
> <u>All</u> their attempts . . .
>
> <u>Those</u> attempts . . .

Helping students recognize determiners as a special kind of noun signaler—that is, in a class apart from the traditional "adjective" label—will help them understand not only the structure of the noun phrase but the structure of the sentence patterns as well.

Auxiliaries. Verbs are so systematic that they can almost be defined on the basis of form alone. But another criterion we can use in discussing and understanding verbs is their affinity with auxiliaries: a verb is a word that can be signaled by auxiliaries, such as *can* and *must* and *should*. Our two most common auxiliaries, *be* and *have,* also meet the criteria for verbs; in fact, they are among our most common verbs. In other words, they belong to both classes: verb and auxiliary. The auxiliary *do* (which we use for negative sentences and questions when there is no other auxiliary) also fits into both classes. *Do* is a verb in the sentence *He does that very well;* it is an auxiliary (and *swim* is the verb) in the negative sentence *He does not swim well* and the question *Does he swim well?*

In traditional grammar, all of the auxiliaries are considered verbs. But when you consider the criterion of form, it's obvious that modal auxiliaries such as *can* and *must* and *should* do not belong to the verb class: they have no *-s* and *-ing* forms, and they do not take other auxiliaries.

Qualifiers: Qualifiers are those words that qualify or intensify adjectives and adverbs, such as *very,* our most common qualifier. Others are *too, quite, rather, fairly,* and *awfully.* (Note: In traditional grammar, the qualifiers are included in the definition of an adverb.) Because some adverbs of manner, the *-ly* adverbs, are themselves used to qualify adjectives (*especially* difficult, *absolutely* true, *dangerously* close), the qualifier class, like that of the determiners, is not a closed class. It can be thought of as both a word class and a sentence function.

Definitions of the Form Classes

Here, then, are definitions of the four form classes based on form, as well as on the structure words that signal them and their function in the sentence:

> *Noun:* A word that may be made plural and/or possessive; it may have a derivational suffix, such as *-tion, -ment,* or *-ness;* it fills the headword position in the noun phrase; it is generally signaled by a determiner.
>
> *Verb:* A word that can have both an *-s* and an *-ing* ending; it can be signaled by auxiliaries and modified by adverbials.
>
> *Adjective:* A word that may take *-er* and *-est* (or *more* and *most*). It may have a derivational suffix, such as *-ous, -ful, -ish,* and *-ive.* It can be marked by a qualifier, such as *very.* It functions as a modifier of nouns; it can fill the role of subject complement and object complement.
>
> *Adverb:* Like the adjective, it may also take an *-er* and *-est* ending (or *more* and *most*); it often ends in *-ly.* It adds such information as time, place, and manner. It can be signaled by qualifiers, such as *very.* It can occupy many different positions in the sentence.

Sentence Constituents

We can use form to help identify sentence constituents, just as we did with words. We begin by considering the two basic units of the sentence, the *noun phrase* and the *verb phrase.* Here is the formula for the two main sentence constituents, as modern linguists generally describe them:

$$S = NP + VP$$
The boy slept in the tent = The boy + slept in the tent.

These terms, of course, refer to forms. Using terms referring to functions, we would say that the two basic units of the sentence are the *subject* and the *predicate.* We begin our discussion with the noun phrase (NP), which has an easy-to-spot characteristic form. Then we look at the other basic sentence constituent, the verb phrase (VP).

Chapter 8

The Noun Phrase

The term *noun phrase* is not one that is used in traditional school grammar, so it may be unfamiliar to you and your students. *Phrase* traditionally refers to a group of words that functions as a unit within the sentence; however, because a single word can function as a unit *(Dogs bark; Felipe laughed)*, we will alter the traditional definition to include single words: *A phrase is a word or group of words that functions as a unit within the sentence.* A phrase will always have a head, or *headword*; the headword of a noun phrase is, of course, a noun. Most noun phrases also include the noun signaler we discussed in the section The Structure Classes—the *determiner.*

We saw the sentence in terms of a formula; we can look at the NP in the same way:

NP = Det + NOUN
The boy = the + boy

We know, of course, that the noun can have modifiers of various forms. We add them to the formula, using parentheses to indicate that they are optional; that is, a noun phrase is grammatical without them. The two required slots in the NP are the determiner and the noun headword. While it's true that not all nouns require determiners, as the two previous sample sentences show *(Dogs bark; Felipe laughed)*, it's useful to think in terms of the determiner as the opening slot in the NP. (Linguists refer to NPs such as *Dogs* and *Felipe* as having a "zero determiner.") When we come to a determiner, we know we are at the opening of a noun phrase.

NP = Det + (adj) + (n) + NOUN + (prepositional + phrase)
(participial + (relative
phrase)   clause)

NP = a + (small) + (race) + car + (with a red stripe) + (zooming by) + (that I saw)

The structure of the NP provides a good example of the systematic nature of our grammar. When we add modifers, we do so in an established way. In preheadword position, we can add both adjectives and nouns as modifiers, but only in that order:

the <u>industrious grammar</u> students
Det   adj   n   NOUN

In postheadword position, we can add prepositional phrases, participial phrases, and relative clauses (also called adjectival, or adjective, clauses)—always in that order:

the students <u>in our school</u> <u>participating in the 10K race</u>
Det NOUN   prep phr   participial phrase

<u>who were excused from class</u>
relative clause

Most noun phrases will not have all of these modifiers, but all are certainly possible. And all of them can be compounded, or multiplied. In the case of the prenoun, or single-word modifiers, compounding is especially common: the *little old* man; the *beautiful, fluffy white* cat. Those modifiers can themselves have modifiers: the *absolutely perfect* birthday present. And we've all seen the problem of proliferating nouns as modifiers: *the faculty committee conference report*—and, if there are errors in that report, *the faculty committee conference report errors*!

All of these various forms of modifiers in the NP are functioning as *adjectivals;* in other words, they are functioning as adjectives function. The NP formula clearly illustrates that many different forms can function as noun modifiers, not just adjectives. In a phrase such as *the baseball player,* rather than label *baseball* an adjective, as the traditional grammarian might, we would look at both its form and its function: *baseball* is a noun in form, an adjectival in function. The traditional definition of *adjective*—a word that modifies a noun—is essentially a definition of *adjectival.*

The NP itself fills many roles in the sentence, functions known as *nominals:* subject, direct object, indirect object, subject complement, object complement, object of preposition, and appositive.

Subject: *The bird* is singing.

Direct object: He bought *the bird* in Florida.

Indirect object: He gave *the bird* a bell to play with.

Subject complement: She is *a bird* when it comes to eating.

Object complement: She called her pet *"Bird."*

Object of preposition: The cat is actually scared of *the bird.*

Appositive: Janice, his *bird*, cheers up the whole apartment.

Writers who understand the form and function of NPs will have a great deal of the sentence under control. We examine these roles in the description of sentence patterns.

There are a number of ways to encourage students to use and understand their own linguistic expertise in the study of noun phrases. Determining where the subject NP ends and the predicate begins, for example, will not be a problem, even when the subject NP includes post-headword modifiers:

The students from our school participating in the race made us all proud.

Students can easily find the line between NP and VP, between subject and predicate, by substituting a pronoun for the subject:

They made us all proud.

Even those non-native speakers who may have had only moderate experience with English will recognize that the personal pronoun stands in for the entire NP, not just the noun headword. Pointing out this grammar rule will certainly be of value to the ESL speaker. The following pronoun test can be used to identify any nominal that fills an NP slot, not just noun phrases: verb phrases and clauses can also function as nominals:

What you do with your money is none of my business.
    That   is none of my business.

I really enjoy *running around the track every morning.*
I really enjoy   *it.*

There are many ways in which NP lessons can be used to help students with their writing. The students can be asked, for example, to find and evaluate the expanded NPs in their assigned readings, perhaps even distinguishing different writers on the basis of their NP styles. They can look for NPs in their own writing, or in that of their peers during group work, that could be enhanced with modifiers. Sometimes, of course, the opposite instruction may be more appropriate: Find a more precise noun, one that makes those added modifiers unnecessary.

Once students have learned how to identify noun phrases, they can learn more about the characteristics of some of the components of those phrases:

1. Movable Participles

Participles are the forms of the verb ending in *-ing* (the present participle) and *-ed* or *-en* (the past participle) and used in verb phrases *(The baby is sleeping)*, as well as to modify nouns, as discussed here. The postheadword slot in the NP, immediately after the noun, can be thought of as the home base for the participial phrase. (Single-word participles will usually be in the preheadword position, before the noun: the *sleeping* baby. Qualified participles, too, will be in preheadword position, often connected with a hyphen: the *well-worn* phrase.) When a postheadword participial phrase in the subject NP is nonrestrictive—that is, set off by commas—it can be moved: It can open or close the sentence:

> The incumbent, *having collected huge campaign contributions,* won by a landslide.
>
> *Having collected huge campaign contributions,* the incumbent won by a landslide.
>
> The incumbent won by a landslide, *having collected huge campaign contributions.*

The opening position is the more common of the two variations; the end position works only when the sentence is fairly short. Notice that, no matter what the position of the participle is, the relationship of the head-word to the participle is a subject-verb relationship. The writer who understands this concept will recognize the problem of the dangling participle, which sometimes occurs in sentence-opening and -closing positions; the dangling participle is a verb without a subject: *Having collected huge campaign contributions, the election was a landslide.*

2. Movable Adjectives

Although usually a preheadword modifier, the adjective can make a stylistic statement when it is compounded and placed after the head-word:

> The unfamiliar neighborhood, *dark and still,* felt strangely ominous.
>
> The neighborhood, *unusually quiet,* felt strangely ominous.

3. Appositives

Most appositives are NPs in form. In function, an appositive can be thought of as a combination of adjectival and nominal. In the following example, the appositive renames the subject NP *(the old house)*—and could actually substitute for the subject; but it also modifies it by adding descriptive information:

> The old house, *an abandoned Victorian with peeling paint,* adds to the ominous feeling of the neighborhood.

Many of the *be* sentences that students so often overuse can be revised when the writers recognize that the NPs in subjective complement position after that linking *be* can be turned into appositives. The complement in the following sentence is the source of the appositive in the previous one:

> The old house is *an abandoned Victorian with peeling paint.*

4. Absolute Phrases

One of the most sophisticated of stylistic devices (and probably the one least used by student writers) is the absolute phrase—an NP in form, with one postnoun modifier, commonly a participle, following the head-word. A tight, controlled modifier, it sends a message to the reader: "Pay attention! I constructed this sentence carefully."

> The abandoned Victorian house added a note of seedy gentility to the neighborhood, *its paint peeling, its gingerbread scrollwork edging the eaves like lace.*
>
> *His nose constantly in a book,* my brother has no interest in competitive sports.

These two examples of the absolute phrase offer a detail or point of focus to the idea stated in the main clause. Another kind of absolute explains a cause or condition:

> *The snowstorm showing no signs of abating,* school was cancelled for the third day in a row.
>
> *A well-regulated militia being necessary to the security of a free state,* the right of the people to keep and bear arms shall not be infringed.

(Note that this rendering of the second amendment does not include two commas that appear in the original: one following *militia* and one following *arms.* Punctuation conventions have changed in the past two centuries.)

As you can see from this short description, an understanding of the NP can provide the framework for a great deal of sentence grammar.

The Verb Phrase

The VP or verb phrase in the linguist's formula (S = NP + VP) is, of course, the predicate. The form of the predicate will be determined to a great extent by the class of the verb: linking, intransitive, or transitive. The one-word predicates in our earlier sample sentences *(Dogs bark; Felipe laughed)* are obviously intransitive verbs because the intransitive class is the only one in which we find verbs that require no complements in order to be grammatical. The other classes require either adjectivals and/or nominals as complements.

Like the noun phrase, the verb phrase too can be described as a formula; for example, V + NP represents the predicate of the basic transitive sentence, such as,

> Felipe *bought a new car.*
>
> The students *have finished their homework.*

The VP almost always includes a *finite verb* that shows whether the VP is in the past or present tense. The finite verb in a VP can be identified in two ways: it is in either the past or present tense, and it appears at the front of the VP (or as the main verb itself if the verb phrase consists of only one verb). Thus, in the previous examples, the finite verbs are *bought*, in the past tense and the only verb, and the auxiliary *have*, the present tense of the verb *to have*, at the front of the VP *have finished.*

Verb phrases that do not indicate tense are called *nonfinite.* The VPs we saw as modifiers in the noun phrase, participles, are among these nonfinite verbs. The other two classes of nonfinite verbs are gerunds, which end in *-ing* and function as nominals (as in *Buying a car is exciting*), and infinitives, which are usually preceded by *to* (as in *I want to finish my homework soon*). Participles, gerunds, and infinitives are known as *verbals.* Verbals, standing by themselves, do not indicate past or present time, so we call them nonfinite verbs.

All VPs, finite and nonfinite, have in common the ability to be modified by *adverbials,* which can take the form of single words, phrases, or clauses. We should note that the traditional definition of *adverb* is (in part) actually the definition of *adverbial:* a word that modifies a verb. There are five different forms that function as adverbials, as modifiers of the verb:

1. adverb (We walked *quickly*.)
2. noun phrase (We went to the movies *last night*.)
3. prepositional phrase (We went *to the movies*.)
4. verb phrase (We walked to the store *to buy a frozen pizza for dinner*.)
5. clause (We walked to the store *because the car wouldn't start*.)

It is not only their variety of form that makes the adverbials such useful tools for the writer; it is also their movability. Adverbials can open or close the sentence, depending on the writer's focus (*Last night, we went to the movies; We went to the movies last night*). They can also appear in the middle of the sentence, between the subject and the predicate, or between the verb and the complement, positions in which they are often set off by commas—and call attention to themselves (*All three of us, because we studied hard, got A's for the course*). Adverbials are versatile in purpose as well, adding, as they do, information of time and place and manner, reason, and the like.

Sentence Patterns

The seven sentence patterns described here represent the bare bones of perhaps 95 percent or more of our sentences. We should note also that a more accurate term would be *verb phrase pattern;* the seven categories are determined by variations in the predicates—in the verb headword and the slots that follow it. We should note, too, that all verb phrases, both finite and nonfinite, will have the complements and can also have the adverbials that predicates of sentences have.

Recognizing that all sentences can, and often do, include adverbials of various forms, we include an adverbial slot (ADV) in the sentence pattern formulas. As with the NP formula, the parentheses can be translated as "optional"; we must note, however, that in many sentences the adverbials provide the new, important information, the reason for the sentence. And we have a few verbs in both the intransitive and transitive categories that require adverbial information for the sentence to be grammatical:

My parents *reside in Arizona.* (intransitive)

She *put* the book *on the shelf.* (transitive)

Here, then, are the seven basic patterns, distinguished by the class of the verb—whether linking, intransitive, or transitive—and the slots that follow the verb. It's also important to recognize that the slots labeled NP are actually nominal slots; they can be filled by forms other than noun phrases—that is, by infinitives, gerunds, and nominal clauses.

Linking Verbs

1. NP	V-link	ADJ	(ADV)
The teacher	seems	tired	today.
SUBJECT		SUBJECT COMPLEMENT	

2. NP¹	V-link	NP¹	(ADV)
The students	are	a boisterous bunch.	
SUB		SUB COMP	

(The identical superscript numbers on the two NPs in pattern 2 denote that the NPs have the same referent; in other words, *the students* and *a boisterous bunch* refer to the same people. The subject complement describes [when an adjective] or renames [when an NP] the subject. Other common linking verbs include *become, remain,* and the verbs of the senses: *taste, feel, smell, look.*)

Intransitive Verbs

3. NP	Verb-intr	(ADV)
Felipe	walked	to school.
SUB		

Transitive Verbs

4. **NP¹**	**V-trans**	**NP²**	**(ADV)**
The students	studied	their history lesson.	
SUB		DIRECT OBJECT	

(The superscript numbers provide an almost infallible way of determining that the NP following the verb is a direct object; unlike the subject complement, the direct object has a referent different from that of the subject, so here the number is different. The traditional definition of the direct object—"receiver of the action"—is not always accurate.)

5. **NP¹**	**V-trans**	**NP²**	**NP³**	**(ADV)**
The teacher	gave	the students	a big assignment	this morning.
SUB		INDIRECT OBJ	DIR OBJ	

(The subgroup of transitive verbs that take indirect objects have a "give"-like meaning: *present, award, deliver, issue, provide, bequeath.* The indirect object is the recipient of the direct object. Note that all three NP slots have different referents.)

6. **NP¹**	**V-trans**	**NP²**	**ADJ**	**(ADV)**
The teacher	considers	the students	very capable.	
SUB		DIR OBJ	OBJECT COMPLEMENT	

7. **NP¹**	**V-trans**	**NP²**	**NP²**	**(ADV)**
The students	elected	Felipe	class president	yesterday.
SUB		DIR OBJ	OBJ COMP	

(Other members of this subgroup of transitive verbs that can take an object complement include *find, make,* and *prefer.* The relationship of direct object to object complement is like the relationship of subject complements to subjects in the linking category: the direct object and object complement have the same referent. Note that in spite of having three NPs, this pattern is easily distinguished from pattern 5, in which all three NPs have different referents.)

It's important to recognize that many verbs have variations in meaning that may put them into more than one of these patterns:

We *grew* tomatoes last summer in the garden. (*transitive*)

I *grew* fat in the winter. (*linking*)

The kittens *grew* fast. (*intransitive*)

Clearly, it's not only the verb that determines the sentence pattern; we must also consider the structures that fill the predicate slots.

The Verb System of African American English

The sentence *Mary be happy*, which was discussed in Chapter 2, illustrates one of the most noticeable differences between Standard English and African American English: the construction of verb strings. Both systems use forms of *have* and *be* and *do* as auxiliaries, but they do so in different ways. Following is a partial list of common AAE verb strings, along with the Standard English equivalent for each (Green)*:

1. He eat. (present) / He is eating.
2. He be eating. (habitual) / He is usually eating.
3. He been eating. (remote past) / He has been eating for a long time.
4. He been ate. (remote past) / He ate a long time ago.
5. He done ate. (completive) / He has already eaten.
6. He been done ate. (remote past completive) / He finished eating a long time ago.
7. He had done ate. (completive) / He has already eaten.

We can recognize certain regular features of the system from this small sample:

- The auxiliary *done* appears in all the completive forms. Note that the adverb *already* or the verb *finished* is required to express the Standard English equivalent.

- The auxiliary *been* (pronounced "bin" and spoken with strong stress) carries the meaning of remote time. The Standard English equivalent requires "a long time" or "a long time ago" to make this remote past distinction.

- The habitual *be*, shown in the second example, includes the meaning of "usually" or "habitually," whereas in Standard English the adverb must be supplied.

It should be obvious from this brief description that the verb forms of AAE, although different from those of Standard English, are produced by a highly systematized set of rules. This recognition should also reinforce the important lesson discussed earlier: that all varieties of English are equally grammatical.

---

*This section on the verb system of African American English is adapted from Martha Kolln and Robert Funk's *Understanding English Grammar,* 6th ed. (New York: Longman, 2002), which is in turn adapted from Lisa Green's article "Study of Verb Classes in African American English," *Linguistics and Education* 7 (1995), pp. 65–81.

Conclusion

The introduction of this book asked several questions about the role of grammar in the language arts and English classroom. This conclusion summarizes some of the answers.

How can we teach grammar to support learning in all language skills? If you think of the grammar that you teach as a language about language, then grammar is useful any time you discuss particular words or sentences with your students. The formal term for this language-about-language is *metalanguage,* a vocabulary about language itself, one that makes it possible for us to redirect our words back on themselves so that we can talk and write about how we talk and write. As with any new type of language, you and your students will need some time to get used to it. But it is as handy—and necessary—in order to discuss what makes a sentence the way it is as the terms for science and mathematics are for talking about an experiment or a problem.

How can we teach grammar so that students discover its rules and principles on their own instead of hearing us impose those rules and principles on them? Grammar is a tricky word. On the one hand, it means "the language of language." On the other hand, you may need to remind yourself from time to time that all of us are grammar experts: we all know grammar; we all know how to maneuver words and phrases in order to communicate effectively nearly all the time. We also are all keen observers of language. We see and hear the kinds of language that people use in different situations. The teacher's challenge is to tap into all this expertise. You may want to consciously practice a repertoire of a few flexible questions and directions that can help elicit points of grammar in many different classroom discussions:

- "How would you say [or write] this in a certain situation, with a certain audience? How have you heard other people say it?"
- "Find examples of [a phrase, a type of sentence, a construction, etc.] in someone's writing or in conversation."
- "What is the pattern in these examples?"
- "What could the rule or definition be? Test it out on another example."

The last two questions asked in the introduction are: *How can we teach grammar so that we strengthen rather than undermine our efforts to honor the voices and cultures of all students? How can we teach grammar so that the knowledge it provides can help learners feel confident about their own language and appreciate the languages of others?* The answers to these questions take us back to a third definition of the word *grammar*—or at least a third aspect of it, besides its definitions as a metalanguage and as each person's ability to arrange words meaningfully. This third aspect is that all languages and language varieties have grammar. They all follow patterns, in other words. This is the foundation of understanding language and of understanding even the conventions of Standard English usage and punctuation. You need to grasp the universality of grammar clearly enough so that when a student speaks in a nonstandard idiom, when a second language student produces a strange-sounding phrase, or when a student paper reveals a repeated error, you can respond to the richness of the language patterns and not just to the absence of a particular one. With grammar, the glass is always half full.

A Grammar Glossary

If you think your understanding of grammatical terminology may be a bit rusty, then this glossary should be helpful. It defines familiar terms (such as *adjective*) and some not quite as familiar (such as *adjectival*) and gives examples. It is not intended to be a complete grammar glossary. More complete descriptions can be found in Martha Kolln and Robert Funk's *Understanding English Grammar* and other grammar texts.

Absolute phrase: A noun phrase with one modifier, often a participial phrase, following the noun headword. An absolute phrase can explain a cause or condition, as in *The temperature having dropped suddenly, we decided to build a fire in the fireplace,* or it can add a detail or a point of focus, as in *The children rushed out the schoolhouse door, their voices filling the playground with shouts of freedom.*

Active voice: A feature of sentences in which the subject performs the action of the verb and the direct object is the goal or the recipient: *The mechanic fixed the car.* See also **Passive voice.**

Adjectival: Any structure (word, phrase, or clause) that fills the role of an adjective—that is, that functions as an adjective normally does, modifying a noun: *The house on the corner is new.* In this sentence, *on the corner* is an adjectival prepositional phrase.

Adjective: A form-class word that functions as a noun modifier. Adjectives can be made comparative and superlative *(tall, taller, tallest)* and can be qualified or intensified *(very tall).*

Adverb: A form-class word that generally modifies a verb, as in *I will be going soon.* Adverbs can also modify the sentence as a whole, as in *Unfortunately, I was out when you phoned.* Some adverbs can be compared (more *quickly*) or intensified (very *quickly*). Their position in the sentence is often flexible *(I will soon be going; Soon I will be going).*

Adverbial: Any structure (word, phrase, or clause) that functions as a modifier of a verb—that is, that fills the role of an adverb. In *We drove to the airport to pick up Uncle Louie, to the airport* is an adverbial prepositional phrase and *to pick up Uncle Louie* is an adverbial infinitive phrase, both modifying the verb *drove.*

Affix: A meaningful unit that is added to the beginning (prefix) or end (suffix) of a word to change its meaning or its function or its part of speech: (prefix) *unhelpful;* (suffix) *unhelpful.* See also **Prefix; Suffix.**

Agreement: See **Pronoun-antecedent agreement; Subject-verb agreement.**

Antecedent: The word or phrase, usually a noun phrase, that a pronoun stands for: *Here is your present. I hope that you like it.*

Appositive: A structure that adds information by renaming another structure, as in *Ginger, my dog, is sweet but stubborn.* Or, *My daily exercise routine, running around the track, sometimes gets very boring.*

Article: The determiners *a* and *an* (the indefinite articles) and *the* (the definite article): *A View to a Kill; The Man with the Golden Gun.*

Auxiliary verb: A structure-class word used with verbs. Auxiliary verbs include *have, be,* and *do* when they are used in phrases with other verbs, as well as such modals as *will* and *must: Miguel will have left by tomorrow. Do you need to see him?* See also **Modal.**

Base form of the verb: The uninflected form of the verb, as it appears in the frame "To ___ is difficult." The base form appears in the infinitive *(To be or not to be)*, in the present tense for all persons except third-person singular *(I walk, you walk, we walk, they walk)*, and in other verb phrases *(He must walk; They will walk).*

Case: A feature of nouns and certain pronouns (personal and relative pronouns) that is determined by the role the noun or pronoun fills in the sentence. Pronouns have three case distinctions: subjective (for example, *he, we, who*), possessive *(his, our, whose)*, and objective *(him, us, whom)*. Nouns have only one case inflection, the possessive *(John's, the cat's)*. See also **Objective case; Subjective case.**

Clause: A sequence of words that includes a subject and a predicate: *Ellen slept; Ellen dreamed about her daughter, who was away at school.* See also **Dependent clause; Independent clause.**

Coherence: The quality of being orderly, logical, and consistent. See also **Cohesion.**

Cohesion: The grammatical and semantic connections between sentences and paragraphs. Cohesive ties are furnished by pronouns that have antecedents in previous sentences, by adverbial connections, by known information, by repeated or related words, and by knowledge shared by the reader.

Comma splice: Two independent clauses joined by a comma, as in *Juana went home, she has a doctor's appointment for her son.* See also **Run-on sentence.**

Complement: A structure that completes the predicate, such as a direct object *(She planted roses)*, indirect object *(He gave her a kiss)*, subject complement *(He became sleepy)*, and object complement *(She named him Theodore).*

Complex sentence: A sentence consisting of one independent, or main, clause and at least one dependent clause, as in *Computers are frustrating when they don't work.*

Compound-complex sentence: A sentence consisting of two or more independent clauses and at least one dependent clause, as in *Computers are frustrating when they don't work, but we all use them anyway.*

Compound sentence: A sentence consisting of two or more independent, or main, clauses, as in *Computers are frustrating sometimes, but we all use them anyway.*

Conjunction: A structure-class word that connects two or more words, phrases, or clauses. See also **Conjunctive adverb; Coordinating conjunction; Correlative conjunction; Subordinating conjunction.**

Conjunctive adverb: A conjunction with an adverbial emphasis (*however, therefore, nevertheless, moreover,* etc.) that connects two clauses, as in *Chocolate is delicious; <u>however</u>, I try my best to stay away from it.*

Coordinating conjunction: A conjunction that connects two words, phrases, or clauses as equals: *and, but, or, nor, for,* and *yet.* For example, *Abraham <u>and</u> Jeff worked Tuesday.*

Correlative conjunction: A two-word conjunction: *either–or; neither–nor; both–and; not only–but also.* For example, *<u>Neither</u> the sofa <u>nor</u> that table looks right in this corner.*

Dangling participle: A participial phrase at the beginning or end of a sentence in which the subject of the sentence is not the subject of the participle. In other words, a dangling participle is a verb without a subject, as in *<u>Walking through the woods</u>, the moon shone brightly.*

Declarative sentence: A sentence in the form of a statement (in contrast to a command, a question, or an exclamation): *April showers bring May flowers.*

Dependent clause: A clause that fills a role in a sentence (such as adverbial, adjectival, or nominal) and that cannot stand independently as a sentence: *He climbed <u>until he was exhausted</u>* (adverbial clause); *I wonder <u>where I put my keys</u>* (nominal clause functioning as direct object). See also **Independent clause.**

Determiner: A structure-class word that marks or signals a noun, appearing as the first word in a noun phrase, before the noun and before any modifiers in the phrase. Determiners include the articles *a, an,* and *the* and those words that can be used in their place: demonstrative pronouns, indefinite pronouns, numbers, possessive pronouns, and possessive nouns. For example, *<u>The</u> telephone is <u>a</u> wonderful invention; <u>This</u> darned telephone doesn't work; <u>Some</u> cell phones are expensive; We have <u>three</u> blue, cordless telephones; You're using <u>my</u> cell phone; <u>Conchita's</u> phone doesn't work anymore.*

Direct object: A noun phrase or other nominal structure that names the goal or receiver of the action of the verb, as in *Phil bought <u>a used motorcycle</u>; I enjoy <u>watching basketball</u>; I hope <u>that it doesn't rain tomorrow</u>.* See also **Indirect object.**

Exclamatory sentence: A sentence that expresses excitement or emotion. It may include a shift in word order and is usually punctuated with an exclamation point, as in *What a beautiful day we're having!*

Expletive: A word without semantic meaning used as a placeholder to fill the subject position at the beginning of an independent clause: <u>*It*</u> *is raining;* <u>*There*</u> *is a fly in my soup.*

Finite: Specific, or finite, as to tense. Verbs in the present tense or past tense are finite verbs: *He <u>filled</u> the tub.* Phrases with such verbs are finite verb phrases. In most finite verb phrases, the first verb is the only finite verb: *He <u>had</u> filled the tub.* (*Filled* in this sentence is a past participle.) Modals, which begin many verb phrases, are not as clear as to their finiteness. They don't take endings that indicate the past or present tense, but some of them suggest past, present, or future time as well as possibility or probability. For example, *She can go* can refer to the present or future but not the past. See also **Nonfinite; Modal; Participle.**

Form: The inherent features of grammatical units, as distinguished from their function. The forms of certain word classes are characterized by prefixes and suffixes. The forms of phrases are characterized by headwords and their objects, complements, or modifiers. The forms of clauses are characterized by subjects and predicates. See also **Function.**

Form-class words: The four large classes of words that contribute the lexical content of the language: nouns, verbs, adjectives, and adverbs. They are also called *content words.* Each takes characteristic prefixes and suffixes that distinguish its form. New form-class words appear frequently, and they are sometimes called *open-class words* for this reason. See also **Structure-class words.**

Fragment: A group of words that, although punctuated as if it were a sentence, is not a complete sentence. Some fragments are dependent clauses: *She drove frantically to the store. <u>Because she had run out of bread for tomorrow's lunches.</u>* Others are phrases, without a subject and complete verb: *She went to get bread for tomorrow's lunches. <u>Driving frantically to the store.</u>* While most fragments are the result of punctuation or structural error, they can be used purposefully by experienced writers for stylistic reasons.

Function: The role of a word, phrase, or clause in a sentence. Consider the sentence *To wear a winter coat in the summer is bizarre behavior. To wear a winter coat in the summer* is an infinitive verb phrase that functions as the subject of the sentence. *Winter* in *winter coat* is a noun that functions adjectivally, modifying *coat. In the summer* is a prepositional phrase that functions as an adverbial modifier of *to wear.*

Gerund: An *-ing* verb functioning as a nominal—that is, as a noun functions: *I enjoy <u>reading</u>; <u>Playing</u> the piano is relaxing.* See also **Gerund phrase.**

Gerund phrase: A gerund together with all of its complements and modifiers, as in *Playing the piano is relaxing.* See also **Gerund.**

Headword: The main word of a phrase, the one that the others modify or complement. In the sentence *The boys in the parade waved to the crowd*, *boys* is the headword of the noun phrase *The boys in the parade; in* is the headword of the prepositional phrase *in the parade;* and *waved* is the headword of the verb phrase *waved to the crowd.*

Helping verb: See **Auxiliary verb.**

Imperative: A sentence in the form of a direction or a command; the subject, *you*, is usually deleted, as in *Turn left at the light; Come here; Be quiet.*

Independent clause: The main clause of a sentence, one that can stand on its own: *The house that used to look run down is now painted a bright blue.* See also **Dependent clause.**

Indirect object: The noun phrase naming the recipient of the direct object. Indirect objects can be shifted into prepositional phrases with *to* or *for*, as in *Samantha gave her father a ticket; Samantha gave a ticket to her father.*

Infinitive: The base form of the verb often preceded by *to: To die, to sleep;* / *To sleep: perchance to dream; ay, there's the rub.* See also **Infinitive phrase.**

Infinitive phrase: The infinitive together with all of its complements and modifiers. Infinitive phrases function as adverbials, adjectivals, and nominals: *Rajesh wants to watch his favorite TV show* (infinitive phrase as direct object). See also **Infinitive.**

Inflection: See **Inflectional suffix.**

Inflectional suffix: A suffix added to a noun (*-s* plural, *'s* possessive), verb (*-s*, *-ed, -ing*), or adjective and adverb (*-er* comparative, *-est* superlative) that alters its grammatical role or meaning: *Dog, dogs; Sing, sang.*

Interrogative: A structure-class word that introduces questions and certain nominal clauses: *where, when, who, what, why*, and *how.* For example, *Why is she leaving?; I wonder why she is leaving.*

Interrogative sentence: A sentence in the form of a question (in contrast to a statement, exclamation, or command): *When are we leaving?*

Intransitive verb: A verb that has no complement, although it may take an adverbial modifier: *Denzel's parents arrived at the airport.* See also **Transitive verb.**

Irregular verb: A verb that does not form its past tense and past participle by adding *-ed, -d*, or *-t*, as regular verbs do: *Sing, sang, sung; go, went, gone.* See also **Regular verb.**

Linking verb: A verb that links the complement to the sentence subject, as in *The chicken is tasty; The salad looks delicious; The chef just became my husband.*

Main clause: See **Independent clause.**

Main verb: The verb that fills the last position in the main verb string, or the only position if there are no auxiliary verbs. Sometimes called the *lexical verb*, it carries the specific meaning about actions, events, or states of being, as in *Raheem has been <u>writing</u> a short story. He <u>told</u> me about it.* See also **Auxiliary verb; Main verb string.**

Main verb string: The part of the sentence consisting of the main verb and any auxiliary verbs that precede it: *Tyrone <u>tried</u> hard; Sheila <u>should have been trying</u> harder.* See also **Auxiliary verb; Main verb.**

Modal: An auxiliary verb that opens a main verb string and that conveys the probability, possibility, obligation, or other mood of the main verb. The principal modals are *can, could, will, would, shall, should, may, might,* and *must: He <u>should</u> be here. He said he <u>would</u> be. He <u>must</u> be sick.* Other kinds of modals include *need* and *dare,* as in *You <u>need</u> not have said that* and *I don't <u>dare</u> say it.* Modal phrases include *had to,* as in *Anita <u>had to</u> leave.* See also **Auxiliary verb; Main verb string.**

Modifier: A word, phrase, or clause that adds information about a noun or verb or the sentence as a whole: *The <u>blue</u> chair <u>that I bought at the auction</u> needs painting; The tomatoes grow <u>fast</u> <u>when the nights are warm</u>; <u>Unfortunately</u>, she lost her job.*

Nominal: A word, phrase, or clause that functions as noun phrases do. Nominals do not necessarily contain nouns: *<u>Traveling</u> can be hard work; I'll accept <u>whoever volunteers</u>.* See also **Noun phrase; Nominal clause.**

Nominal clause: A clause that functions as a noun phrase does, often a *that* clause or an interrogative clause, as in *I know <u>that she knows</u>; Denise wondered <u>why they were late</u>.*

Nonfinite: Not definite as to tense. The nonfinite verbs are infinitives, participles, and gerunds. Nonfinite verbs appear in the main verb phrase, where they are preceded by a finite verb (one with tense), as in *Melissa is <u>running</u> in the race* (present participle). They also appear in other phrases where they function nominally, adjectivally, or adverbially; such phrases are nonfinite verb phrases: *Yuri loves <u>to sing</u>* (infinitive); *The <u>snoring</u> man is next door* (present participle); *She likes <u>riding</u> roller coasters* (gerund). See also **Finite.**

Nonrestrictive modifier: A modifier—a word, phrase, or clause—in the noun phrase that comments on the noun but is not necessary for defining or identifying it. It is set off with commas: *The Finance Committee, <u>which met last week</u>, is still working on the budget.* See also **Restrictive modifier.**

Noun: A form-class word that can usually be made plural or possessive, as in *boy, boys, boy's.* Nouns fill the headword slot in noun phrases *(my old Kentucky <u>home</u>)*; they can also serve as adjectivals *(the <u>home</u> team)* and adverbials *(They went <u>home</u>).*

Noun phrase: The noun headword together with all of its modifiers. In the sentence *The gardener trimmed the pine tree with the broken branches, the gardener* is a noun phrase that functions as the sentence subject, and its headword is *gardener*. *The pine tree with the broken branches* is a noun phrase functioning as a direct object, and its headword is *tree*. *The broken branches* is a noun phrase embedded in the longer noun phrase; it functions as the object of the preposition *with,* and its headword is *branches*.

Object complement: A word or phrase in the predicate that completes the idea of the verb and modifies or renames the direct object: *I found the play exciting; We consider Rose Marie a good friend.*

Objective case: The role in a sentence of a noun phrase or pronoun when it functions as an object—direct object, indirect object, object complement, or object of a preposition. Personal pronouns and the relative pronoun *who* have special forms for the objective case: *me, him, her, us,* and *them,* as well as *whom.* For example, *He gave him a stereo for his birthday; Hemingway's For Whom the Bell Tolls is a great novel.*

Object of a preposition: See **Preposition.**

Parallelism: Two or more of the same grammatical structures that are coordinated—given equal weight—within a sentence, as in *He came early and left late; My words went in one ear and out the other.* The term also applies to repeated structures in separate sentences within a paragraph.

Participial phrase: A present or past participle together with its subject or complements and/or modifiers: *Still clutching their pizza in their hands, the kids left the room.* See also **Participle.**

Participle: The verb forms that appear in verb phrases after the auxiliary verbs *to be,* as in *I was eating* (present participle), and *to have,* as in *I have eaten* (past participle). *Participle* is also the term used to refer to the present or past participle in its role as an adjectival, as a modifier in the noun phrase: *The band members, wearing their snazzy new uniforms, proudly marched onto the field.* See also **Present participle; Past participle.**

Particle: Any of various words accompanying the verb as part of a phrasal verb, such as *on* in *catch on* and *up* and *with* in *put up with.*

Passive voice: A feature of sentences in which the object or goal of the action functions as the sentence subject and the main verb phrase includes the verb *to be* and the past participle, as in *The car was fixed by the mechanic.* See also **Active voice.**

Past participle: The form of the verb used in the frame "We have . . . ": *We have forgotten something; We have walked two miles.* The past participle can stand on its own, without *have: Forgotten by his friends, he lived alone.* The past participle is also used with a form of *to be* in the passive voice, as in *The car was fixed by the mechanic.* Even though the past participles that end in *-ed* have the same form as the past tense of regular verbs, the "past" in the name of this verb form does not denote past time: *We have walked* (past participle); *We walked* (past tense); *The dog is walked by the girl next door* (present tense, passive voice). See also **Participle; Present participle.**

Past tense: The *-ed* form of regular verbs, usually denoting an action at a specific time in the past: *They walked down the street.* Irregular verbs have various past tense forms, as in *She bought the car; They took a walk; He was happy.*

Phrasal verb: A verb consisting of a verb plus a particle or particles: *look up* the statistics, *give in* to the pressure, *put up with* the noise, *find out* the truth, *make up* a lie, *turn in* at midnight, *come by* a fortune, *go in* for horse racing, and many other everyday verbs.

Phrase: A word or group of words that functions as a unit in the sentence and is not a clause. *The boy* is a noun phrase. *The boy with the blue shirt* is a noun phrase that includes a prepositional phrase modifying the noun *boy*. *The boy who is mowing the lawn* is a noun phrase that includes an adjectival clause modifying the noun *boy*. See also **Noun phrase; Verb phrase; Preposition; Absolute phrase.**

Predicate: One of the two principal parts of the sentence, it's the comment made about the subject. The predicate includes the verb together with its complements and modifiers: *The building finally collapsed after years of decay*. See also **Subject.**

Predicate adjective: The adjective that functions as a subject complement following a linking verb, as in *He became sleepy*. See also **Linking verb; Subject complement.**

Predicate nominative: The noun or nominal that functions as a subject complement: *She became an engineer*. See also **Linking verb; Subject complement.**

Prefix: A meaningful unit added to the beginning of a word to change its meaning (*illegal*) or its class (*enable*). See also **Affix; Suffix.**

Preposition: A structure-class word that combines with a nominal (the object of the preposition) to form a prepositional phrase, which functions adjectivally or adverbially, as in *On Tuesday, the circus came to town*. Prepositions can be simple (*above, at, in, of, for, from*, etc.) or phrasal (*according to, instead of*, etc.).

Present participle: The form of the verb used with the frame "We are . . .": *We are going; They should be leaving soon*. This *-ing* form of the verb is also used as an adjectival modifier as well as a main verb: *Leaving the park, she was feeling the excitement of the city*. The word *present* in the label for this verb form does not denote present time, and in fact the present participle is not definite as to time: *He is leaving; He was leaving*. See also **Participle; Nonfinite.**

Present tense: The base form *(eat)* along with the *-s* form *(eats)* that is used with a third-person singular subject. The present tense denotes a present point in time *(I like your new hairdo)*, a habitual action *(My parents live in Arizona)*, or the "timeless" present *(The earth revolves around the sun)*.

Progressive: A verb construction consisting of the auxiliary *be* and the present participle, expressing ongoing activity or a temporary state, as in *Jamal is eating; Molly was being silly.*

Pronoun: A word that substitutes for a nominal, as in *Sam tried to stop laughing, but he couldn't do it.* Types of pronouns include demonstrative pronouns *(this, these, that, those)*, personal pronouns *(I, me, it, you,* etc.), indefinite pronouns *(every, everyone, many, any,* etc.), relative pronouns *(who, that, which)*, and reflexive pronouns *(myself, yourself, himself,* etc.).

Pronoun-antecedent agreement: The matching of the number (whether singular or plural) of the pronoun to the number of its antecedent: *The boys did their chores; Each girl did her best.*

Qualifier: A structure-class word that qualifies or intensifies adjectives and adverbs, as in *We worked very hard; Joan was slightly annoyed; It's much colder today.*

Regular verb: A verb that forms the past tense and past participle by the addition of *-ed* (or, in a few cases, *-d* or-*t*) to the base form: *Yesterday, he walked to school; Maria has walked all the way.* See also **Irregular verb.**

Relative clause: A clause introduced by a relative pronoun *(who, which, that)* or a relative adverb *(when, where, why)* that generally functions as an adjectival, as in *The book that you wanted has arrived; The area where I live is densely populated.* The broad reference *which* clause functions as a sentence modifier: *John bought a gas-guzzler, which surprised me.* See also **Subordinate clause.**

Relative pronoun: The pronouns *who, whose, whom, that,* and *which,* used to introduce relative clauses: *The boy who lives here is named Jorge.*

Restrictive modifier: A modifier—a word, phrase, or clause—in the noun phrase that restricts and identifies the meaning of the noun. It is not set off by commas: *Homer's epic poem* The Odyssey *is a great book to teach; The chair that you just sat on is broken.* See also **Nonrestrictive modifier.**

Rhetoric: The aspects of language use and organization that make it effective and persuasive for an audience; the study of those aspects.

Run-on sentence: Two independent clauses with no punctuation between them, as in *Juana went home she has a doctor's appointment for her son.*

Semantics: Meaning in language; the study of meaning in language.

Sentence modifier: A word, phrase, or clause that modifies the sentence as a whole, rather than a particular structure within it. It is sometimes called a *free modifier:* <u>*Ironically,*</u> *the other team won;* <u>*In an ironic turn of events,*</u> *the other team won.*

Simple sentence: A sentence consisting of a single independent clause, as in *Computers can be frustrating.* See also **Complex sentence; Compound sentence; Compound-complex sentence.**

Structure-class words: The classes of words that show the grammatical or structural relationships between form-class words. The major structure classes are conjunctions, prepositions, auxiliaries, determiners, qualifiers, interrogatives, and expletives. New structure-class words appear rarely and for this reason they are referred to as *closed classes.* See also **Form-class words.**

Subject: The opening position in the basic structure of a sentence, filled by a noun phrase or other nominal that functions as the topic of the sentence, as in <u>*This old upright piano*</u> *still sounds beautiful.* See also **Predicate.**

Subject complement: The nominal or adjectival that follows a linking verb and renames or modifies the sentence subject: *Charleston, South Carolina, is* <u>*a beautiful city.*</u> See also **Predicate adjective; Predicate nominative.**

Subjective case: The role of a noun phrase or a pronoun when it functions as the subject of a clause. Personal pronouns have distinctive forms for subjective case: *I, he, she, we, they.* For example, <u>*She*</u> *and Tom are happy.*

Subject-verb agreement: The matching of the number and person of the subject to the form of the verb. When the subject is third-person singular and the verb is in the present tense, the verb takes the *-s* inflection, as in *The dog* <u>*barks*</u> *all night. He* <u>*bothers*</u> *the neighbors.* With other subjects and in other tenses, verbs (with the exception of *be*) do not change to match the number or person of the subject: *I* <u>*sleep*</u>*; we* <u>*sleep*</u>*; he* <u>*slept*</u>*; they* <u>*slept*</u>*.*

Subordinate clause: A dependent clause introduced by a subordinating conjunction such as *if, since, because,* and *although.* Subordinate clauses are usually adverbial: *We left* <u>*because it was getting late.*</u> See also **Dependent clause.**

Subordinating conjunction: A conjunction that introduces a subordinate clause. Among the most common, both simple and compound, are *after, although, as long as, because, before, if, since, so that, provided that, though, until, when, whenever,* and *while.*

Suffix: A meaningful unit added to the end of a word to change its class (*laugh—laugh*<u>*able*</u>), its function (*eat—eat*<u>*ing*</u>), or its meaning (*dog—dog*<u>*s*</u>). See also **Affix; Prefix.**

Syntax: The structure and arrangement of words, phrases, and clauses in sentences; the study of this topic.

Transitive verb: A verb that requires a direct object as its complement to be complete, as in *He* <u>*drove*</u> *the car.* Many verbs can be either transitive or intransitive: *Charles drove*. Most transitive verbs can be made passive: *The car was driven by Charles*. See also **Intransitive verb; Passive voice.**

Verb: A form-class word that names an action, process, event, or state; that can always take both -*s* and -*ing* endings; and that can be signaled by auxiliary verbs: *It goes; She is going; We should go*.

Verbal: Another term given to nonfinite verbs—participles, gerunds, and infinitives—when their function is other than that of main verb: as adjectivals, adverbials, or nominals.

Verb phrase: A verb together with its auxiliaries, modifiers, and complements. The predicate of the sentence is a verb phrase, as in *He left all his belongings, including his guitar, in the house*. The term is sometimes used more narrowly to refer to just the main verb and its auxiliaries. See also **Main verb string.**

Sources and Resources

On the Web

Here are some informative Web sites, most of them from language or-
ganizations:

www.americandialect.org: The site for the American Dialect Society.

www.ateg.org: The Web site for NCTE's Assembly for the Teaching of
English Grammar; it provides a variety of resources for teaching and
learning about grammar.

www.cal.org: The site for the Center for Applied Linguistics.

www.grammarlady.com: Mary Newton Bruder's well-run site.

www.linguistics-online.de: A virtual linguistics "campus" organized by three
German universities (the materials are all in English).

www.lsadc.org: The Web site for the Linguistic Society of America.

www.ucl.ac.uk/internet-grammar: An Internet grammar source from the
major writers on grammar in England.

The other approach to the Internet, of course, is to use a search engine.
It is a good idea to try different search headings; "grammar," "teaching
English grammar," and "grammar lessons" each leads to different search
results.

In Print

Berk, Lynn M. *English Syntax: From Word to Discourse.* New York: Oxford
University Press, 1999. A concise presentation of English syntax and
its links to semantics and discourse function.

Connors, Robert J. "The Erasure of the Sentence." *College Composition and
Communication* 52 (2000): 96–128. The article traces the rise of three
sentence-based pedagogies—Christensen's generative rhetoric,
sentence combining, and sentence imitation—that appeared in the
1960s and 1970s and their fall after 1980 at the hands of antiformalist
and antiempiricist movements in English education.

Crystal, David. *The Cambridge Encyclopedia of Language.* Cambridge, UK:
Cambridge UP, 1997. See next item.

Crystal, David. *The Cambridge Encyclopedia of the English Language*. Cambridge, UK: Cambridge UP, 2001. Two one-volume works with readable, illustrated information on all aspects of language, including traditional and modern grammar. Reasonably priced in their paperbound editions.

DeBeaugrande, Robert. "Forward to the Basics: Getting Down to Grammar." *College Composition and Communication* 35 (1984): 358–67. An early essay arguing for practical approaches to the grammar essentials using the student's native language ability.

English Journal 85.7 (1996) and 92.3 (2003). Two issues of the NCTE journal devoted to articles on teaching grammar.

Garner, Bryan A. *The Oxford Dictionary of American Usage and Style*. New York: Oxford UP, 2000. A well-reasoned guide on questions of current American English grammar, usage, punctuation, and spelling.

Green, Lisa. "Study of Verb Classes in African American English." *Linguistics and Education* 7 (1995): 65–81. An examination of the African American verb classes and some implications for education.

Haussamen, Brock. *Revising the Rules: Traditional Grammar and Modern Linguistics*. 2nd ed. Dubuque, IA: Kendall/Hunt, 2000. Contrasts the history of school grammar rules with recent linguistic perspectives.

Hunter, Susan, and Ray Wallace, eds. *The Place of Grammar in Writing Instruction: Past, Present, Future*. Portsmouth, NH: Boynton/Cook, 1995. Sixteen essays on the past, present, and future of grammar and writing. Includes diverse perspectives from composition teachers, writing center directors, rhetoricians, and others engaged in writing.

Killgallon, Don. *Sentence Composing*. Portsmouth, NH: Boynton/Cook-Heinemann. A series of workbooks for sentence combining, middle school through college.

Kischner, Michael, and Edith Wollin. *Writers' Choices: Grammar to Improve Style*. Fort Worth: Harcourt, 2002. A textbook on using grammatical structures for stylistic effects, with sentence-combining exercises.

Kolln, Martha. *Rhetorical Grammar: Grammatical Choices, Rhetorical Effects*. 4th ed. New York: Longman, 2003. A textbook about the effects of choices of word, structure, and punctuation on such rhetorical qualities as cohesion, emphasis, and tone.

Kolln, Martha, and Robert Funk. *Understanding English Grammar*. 6th ed. New York: Longman, 2002. A comprehensive, clear textbook on English grammar, with Reed-Kellogg sentence diagrams.

Lester, Mark. *Grammar and Usage in the Classroom*. 2nd ed. New York: Allyn and Bacon, 2001. Covers many issues surrounding pedagogical grammar, with traditional Reed-Kellogg diagrams.

Morenberg, Max. *Doing Grammar*. 3rd ed. New York: Oxford UP, 2002. A textbook describing how our internal "grammar machine" arranges sentence constituents.

Morenberg, Max, and Jeff Sommers, with Donald A. Daiker and Andrew Kerek. *The Writer's Options: Lessons in Style and Arrangement.* 6th ed. New York: Longman, 1999. A textbook applying sentence combining to all phases of the writing process, from drafting to revisions for tone and emphasis.

National Council of Teachers of English and International Reading Association. *Standards for the English Language Arts.* Urbana, IL: NCTE, and Newark, DE: IRA, 1996. The twelve standards for teaching English reached after a national study by NCTE and IRA. Includes discussion of student language learning and seventeen teaching vignettes.

Noden, Harry R. *Image Grammar: Using Grammatical Structures to Teach Writing.* Portsmouth, NH: Heinemann, 1999. Concepts and strategies for teaching writing through grammar and its images, from a veteran eighth-grade teacher.

Noguchi, Rei R. *Grammar and the Teaching of Writing: Limits and Possibilities.* Urbana, IL: National Council of Teachers of English, 1991. A guide to a minimal grammar and to student-friendly methods for using one's intuitive sentence sense to find basic sentence components and avoid errors.

Strong, William. *Writer's Toolbox: A Sentence-Combining Workshop.* New York: McGraw-Hill, 1996. A sentence-combining workshop.

Thompson, Geoff. *Introducing Functional Grammar.* London: Arnold, 1996. The approach to grammar through meaning and function rather than structure, originally developed by Michael Halliday in England.

Traugott, Elizabeth Closs, and Mary Louise Pratt. *Linguistics for Students of Literature.* New York: Harcourt Brace Jovanovich, 1980. Although somewhat dated, this textbook provides an effective introduction to the linguistic analysis of literary style.

Weaver, Constance. *Grammar for Teachers: Perspectives and Definitions.* Urbana, IL: National Council of Teachers of English, 1979. Examines how teachers can put their own knowledge of grammar to use in teaching students and introduces traditional, structural, and transformational grammar.

———, ed. *Lessons to Share on Teaching Grammar in Context.* Portsmouth, NH: Boynton/Cook, 1998. Essays by eighteen teachers on teaching grammar in grades K–12.

———. *Teaching Grammar in Context.* Portsmouth, NH: Boynton/Cook, 1996. A survey of the literature on what works and what doesn't work in teaching grammar, with many suggestions for sensible classroom approaches.

Wheeler, Rebecca S., ed. *Language Alive in the Classroom.* Westport, CT: Praeger, 1999. Linguistically based approaches to language varieties and classroom grammar.

Wheeler, Rebecca S., and Rachel Swords. "Codeswitching: Tools of Language and Culture Transform the Dialectally Diverse Classroom." *Language Arts,* in press. National Council of Teachers of English. Research-based techniques from linguistics that foster mastery of Standard English while allowing teachers to honor the students' vernacular language.

Williams, Joseph M. *Style: Ten Lessons in Clarity and Grace.* 6th ed. New York: Longman, 2000. A textbook and guide to grammatical features that improve prose style.

Index

Author and Contributors

Rebecca S. Wheeler, Martha Kolln, Brock Haussamen, and Amy Benjamin.

Brock Haussamen is president of the Assembly for the Teaching of English Grammar and professor of English at Raritan Valley Community College in New Jersey. His previous book is *Revising the Rules: Traditional Grammar and Modern Linguistics* (2000). He has published articles on language and teaching in *Teaching English in the Two-Year College, Visible Language, Death Studies, The Journal of Near-Death Experience,* and *Syntax in the Schools.* At Raritan Valley, where he has taught since 1968, Haussamen teaches courses ranging from developmental English to introductory linguistics. He holds a master's degree in English from the University of Connecticut and a master's in history from Rutgers University.

Amy Benjamin is vice president ATEG and an English teacher at Hendrick Hudson High School in Montrose, New York. She is the author of numerous books, including *Writing in the Content Areas* (1999), *An English Teacher's Guide to Performance Tasks and Rubrics* (2000), and *Differentiated Instruction: A Guide for Middle and High School Teachers* (2002). She is currently at work on a book to be entitled *Understanding Writing Instruction for the 21st Century.* Benjamin works as a consultant for school districts throughout the country and looks forward every year to attending the conference for the Assembly for the Teaching of English Grammar.

Paul E. Doniger is the secretary for ATEG. He teaches English and theater classes and directs the drama program at The Gilbert School, a small semipublic high school in Winsted, Connecticut. Before that, he taught and was head of the English department at a charter high school, called Ancestors, in Waterbury, Connecticut. In addition, he is adjunct professor of English at Western Connecticut State University, from which he holds a Master of Arts in English. He also has taught ESL at the University of Bridgeport. In 1996, Doniger was a co-presenter at the annual ConnTesol conference (on teaching college-level reading to foreign students). Recently, he has written for *English Journal* on using grammar as a tool for teaching literature.

Martha Kolln, a founding member of ATEG, served as the Association's, later Assembly's, president during its first ten years. For the past twenty-five years, she has written and spoken on behalf of grammar as a legitimate, proper, and necessary subject in the language arts curriculum. She retired in 1993 as associate professor from Penn State's English department, where for twenty-two years she taught grammar, composition, rhetorical theory, and editing. Kolln is the author of *Understanding English Grammar* (2002), now in its sixth edition (with Robert Funk), and *Rhetorical Grammar: Grammatical Choices, Rhetorical Effects* (2003), now in its fourth edition.

Helene Krauthamer is associate professor of English at the University of the District of Columbia in Washington, D.C. She holds a Ph.D. and an M.A. in linguistics from the State University of New York at Buffalo and a B.A. in mathematics from New York University. She is current treasurer and past president of the College English Association–Middle Atlantic Group. Her articles have appeared in *Teaching English in the Two-Year College, Journal of Teaching Writing,* and the *CEAMAGazine.* Krauthamer's book, *Spoken Language Interference Patterns in Written English* (1999), analyzes the ways in which speaking influences writing. Her current research interests, in addition to the teaching of grammar, include computers and composition, assessment, and online learning.

Johanna E. Rubba, associate professor, received her M.A. in applied linguistics from Southern Illinois University in Carbondale in 1986 and her Ph.D. in theoretical linguistics from the University of California, San Diego, in 1993. Since 1995 she has been a member of the English department at California Polytechnic State University, San Luis Obispo, where she teaches introductory, upper-division, and graduate courses on a variety of linguistic topics. Most of her students are future K–12 teachers. This and the current emphasis on school reform have motivated Rubba to research and develop curricular materials for grammar instruction based on linguistic science. She has led workshops on grammar teaching at state teacher conferences and has given numerous presentations on grammar teaching at national conferences. She is currently working on a college textbook on the structure of English.

Wanda Van Goor is currently professor of English at Prince George's Community College, Largo, Maryland, where she teaches grammar, composition, and literature. She has also taught at the University of Pennsylvania and as adjunct in the graduate school of George Washington University—and at the University of Hawaii dolphin tanks, where she participated in experiments in teaching grammar to dolphins. She has published in several fields: grammar and usage, literature for teenagers, humanities, housing and urban renewal, community health services, and religion. Books for grammar instruction include *Bedford Basics: A Workbook for Writers*, coauthored with Diana Hacker (1998), and developmental exercises to accompany Hacker's *Rules for Writers, The Bedford Handbook for Writers,* and *A Writer's Reference.* Van Goor's professional conference presentations have ranged from "Respect for the Grammatical Complexity of Children's Books" at the ATEG annual conference and the Children's Literature Association to "Two Straight Lines and More: A Look at the Symmetry of Illustrations, Text, and Grammatical Structure in Ludwig Bemelmans' *Madeline*" at the annual meeting of the International Children' Literature Association in Paris.

Rebecca S. Wheeler is associate professor of English education at Christopher Newport University in Newport News, Virginia. Specializing in language development in urban areas, she brings the insights of contemporary applied linguistics to bear on reducing the achievement gap in dialectally diverse classrooms. Her work on code-switching and contrastive analysis has been hailed as "pioneering" in *District Administration,* and the Newport News public school administration has cited her work as embodying "best practices" in reducing the achievement gap through "breaking the language code." Wheeler is a member of the Linguistic Society of America's Committee on Language in the School Curriculum and has served as editor of *Syntax in the Schools.* Her work is reported in her latest article, "Codeswitching: Tools of Language and Culture Transform the Dialectally Diverse Classroom," to appear in NCTE's *Language Arts.*

Edith Wollin is currently dean of Arts, Humanities, and Adult Basic Education at North Seattle Community College. During her teaching career, she taught English at North Seattle Community College, The Ohio State University, and Concordia College in Moorhead, Minnesota. She is the coauthor of *Writers' Choices: Grammar to Improve Style* (2002) and has published many articles, creative essays, and poems in regional journals. Wollin's major areas of interest include English grammar, Middle English syntax, literature of the American West, and Shakespeare. She holds an M.A. from the University of Kansas, an M.A.T. from the University of Washington, and a Ph.D. from the University of Washington. She is a member of ATEG and NCTE.

This book was typeset in Palatino and Helvetica by Electronic Imaging.
Typefaces used on the cover were Futura Bold and Myriad.
The book was printed on 50-lb. Williamsburg Offset paper by Victor Graphics.